THE POPE AND ME AT YANKEE STADIUM

My Life as the Beer Man & Stand-Up Comic

**by Steve Lazarus
as told to Sandy Miles**

Copyright © 2009 by Steve Lazarus
Updated version 2017
All rights reserved.
No part of this book can be reproduced in any form
without the express written consent of the author.
Copyright Library of Congress 2009
Cover design by Jonathan Morris and FamousVisions.com
Back cover photograph by Howard Simmons
Printed in the United States of America
10 9 8 7 6 5 4 3 2 1
ISBN 0-09820987-0-7

ACKNOWLEDGMENTS

I would like to thank Sandy Miles for his inspiration on this book. Thanks to mom and dad and the rest of my family: brother Berny, sister Judy, nephew Ian, and niece Lauren. Thanks also to my aunts Betty Silver and Evelyn Simon. And still more thanks to my friends Mindy and Mark Levine, Marcy and Jerry Leavitt, and Helaine and Charlie Kobrin. Thanks to Rich Walker for all his support and to Peter Bales and all the comics I've had the pleasure to share the stage with. On the bigger stage, I thank all my fellow vendors I've worked with in the last four decades. Special thanks to Phil Mushnick who always gave me great advice. If I left anyone out, that doesn't mean I don't love you!

*This book is dedicated to our moms,
who always made sure we were safe at home.*

*Like sands through the hourglass,
these are the days of our lives.*

I'm writing an unauthorized autobiography.
—STEVEN WRIGHT

The events in this story take place through the year 2008, the final season at the original Yankee Stadium. (This updated edition includes EXTRA Innings)

FOREWORD

STEVE LAZARUS HAS LONG HELD A JOB no otherwise well-adjusted soul would seek, let alone maintain.

He annually stands with his back to 80-plus Major League Baseball games while demanding $12 payments for cups filled – almost – with 10¢ worth of warming beer.

Such a twisted existence long ago made me a friend, confidant and, above all, an admirer.

But, because life is compensatory – the sightless hear better than the hearing – Lazarus sustains the miserable life he has chosen for himself with an extraordinary sense of humor, honesty, optimism and a pocketful of quarters from those inclined toward tipping for the privilege of being soaked for a couple of sips of barreled beer.

In "The Pope and Me At Yankee Stadium: My Life As The Beer Man & Stand-Up Comic," Lazarus shares with you what he has long shared with me: His rags-to-rags story that will further feed Steve's tragic-comic outlook, not to mention his inevitable ruin, and perhaps a sequel to this book, movie rights, too, maybe.

So join Steve, please, as you travel his unique highway – service roads, actually – bobbing and weaving the slings and arrows of outrageous fortune, now on sale at the concession stand just behind the center field memorial tributes to Babe Ruth and Mickey Mantle.

Any unauthorized use of the play-by-play, other descriptions or laughs generated by the contents of this publication without the expressed written consent of the author are strictly a matter of taste. Arrive home safely.

Phil Mushnick, *New York Post*, 2009

SCORECARD

PRE-GAME SHOW 1

FIRST INNING
  A Bronx Tale 4

SECOND INNING
  Career Opportunities 14

THIRD INNING
  The Start of My Dual Career 25

FOURTH INNING
  Live from New York 37

FIFTH INNING
  All in the Family 57

SIXTH INNING
  A Day in the Life 73

SEVENTH INNING
  All the Wrong Moves 104

EIGHTH INNING
  The Road Taken 122

NINTH INNING
  Coming Full Circle 145

POST-GAME SHOW 148

EXTRA INNINGS
  To Infinity and Beyond 151

PRE-GAME SHOW

OKAY BASEBALL FANS, LISTEN UP!
 Let me set the record straight right off the bat (no pun intended) and tell you the truth: I AM A LIAR.
 All comedians are.
 They say they're single when they're really married. They say they're Ivy League grads when they barely made it out of grade school. They say they've bought a truckload of products from the *Home Shopping Network* but have never heard of the Popeil Pocket Fisherman. They enlighten you with the trials and tribulations of their first sexual encounter, though they happened to be alone at the time.
 This, however, is no fib: sorry Mr. Derek Jeter and Co., but I, alone, comprise the best double-play combination around: Yankee Stadium Beer Man by day, Stand-up Comedian by night.
 Yup, The Fickle Finger of Fate tapped me on the shoulder long before it did Rowan and Martin.
 Sock it to me!

* * *

Back in 1964, two of the hottest things in The City That Never Sleeps were the New York Yankees and *The Soupy Sales Show*. Need I recite chapter and verse the long list of Bronx Bomber Championships even way back then?
 Okay, I will: as of this writing, it's 26 World Championships, 39 American League pennants, and the most storied franchise in sports. Current worth? A *billion* dollars.

1

Need I tell you how often the late Hall of Famer Phil Rizzuto uddered, uh *uttered* the legendary phrase "Holy Cow!" during 1964 and his entire Yankee broadcasting career? Must I tell you how often I'd watch the late Soupy Sales take a custard pie the face from "White Fang," the world's larges dog, or some other zany character from his popular kid's show? Estimates say Soupy's taken one in the kisser a mind-boggling 25,000 times! Could I regale you with the cryptic conversations Soupy had with Fang, who was so large that you only saw his furry paw on screen?

Sure.

But I won't. It's simply enough to say I was hooked on the Yanks and the Soup Man like a fish on a hook. Sports and comedy, what a concept!

Is it any wonder then that I am what I am?

(Save the snide comments.)

Yes, you can say that the stage was set early on.

Soupy and me at the Friars Club in NYC

A year after Soupy Sales hit town and the season after the '64 World Series in which the Yankees lost in seven games to the St. Louis Cardinals, my dad took me to my first game at Yankee Stadium.

THE POPE AND ME AT YANKEE STADIUM

I would stay there for over 40 years.

On October 2, 1979, my third year as a vendor (and long before I was known as The Beer Man), Pope John Paul II visited Yankee Stadium. The place was packed to the rafters. If you asked me how long he stayed that day, I'd have said forever. Some vendors made a small fortune selling souvenirs of the Pope: keychains, necklaces, rings, tee-shirts, you name it, it was for sale. Others did real well selling rosary beads and Holy water. I, however, didn't do too well. I sold hot dogs. *Hebrew National* hotdogs.

The Pope was driven onto the playing field in his "Popemobile," a weird bubble-shaped car that looked a bit like a Double Decker bus.

When I saw the PopeMobile, I remember thinking that I just wanted to push down on the top of it.
Remember that game "Trouble?"
Kacluck! Kacluck! Kacluck!
Hey! It's the Pope-o-matic!

3

FIRST INNING

A Bronx Tale

*I don't get no respect. I joined Gamblers Anonymous.
They gave me two-to-one I wouldn't make it.*

— RODNEY DANGERFIELD

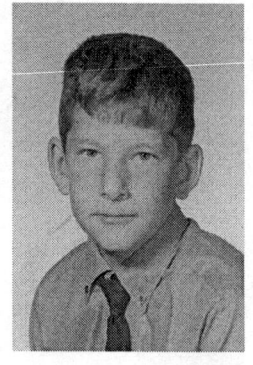

"AND WHAT WOULD YOU LIKE to be when you grow up, Steven?" asked my fourth grade teacher, Mr. Rothman.

"I'd like to work outdoors and feed the hungry."

"That's very nice, Steven."

"Yeah, I want to be a vendor at Yankee Stadium."

My classmates' giggles signaled the beginning of my comedy career.

* * *

I was eight years old when Aaron Lazarus took me to Yankee Stadium for the first time. Despite numerous attempts to persuade my father that the Stadium wasn't located in a Midwestern hayfield accessible only by donning goggles and commandeering a crop duster plane, that it was just on the other side of our house in The Bronx, dad initially wouldn't bite—until fate intervened.

The Yankees, at the start of a decade-long slide after playing in five straight World Series (having won it all in 1961 and '62), still had a bunch of veterans from their glory years including Mickey Mantle, Roger Maris, Whitey Ford, and Elston Howard.

My favorite player was funky and flaky Joe Pepitone. Of course, I wouldn't have thought of making the five-mile trek without my Joe Pepitone Spalding Super Snare glove in tow. Many a glorious day I spent oiling that mitt with anything from mink oil, vaseline, and even some Barbasol shaving cream to make the leather nice and supple. (Dad would've flipped if he knew about the shaving cream.) Then I'd put a softball in it and wrap the glove mummy-like with ace bandages and string and let it set overnight.  I couldn't wait until the next morning to unwrap it and get out onto the makeshift field with my friends to imitate Pepe's slick fielding. It was always nice taking in that aromatic smell of exhaust fumes that wafted in off the Bronx River Parkway!

The Brooklyn-born Pepitone, supposedly the inspiration for John Travolta's character in *Saturday Night Fever*, would gain immortality not so much for his playing days but for his *hairstyling* ways. He was the first baseball player to bring a hairdryer and hairspray into the clubhouse. He may also have been the first to wear a toupee, shoulder length. "I was the first to keep my toupee fashionably long," he once said. Rumor has it that Pepitone had two toupees to cover his quickly balding scalp: one for his time off the field and one that fit "just right" under his baseball cap.

Do you know what Pepitone could've used to keep his hair?
How 'bout a Ziploc bag!

I have heard it said that a complicated childhood can lead to a life in the arts. I tell you this story of my father and me to let you know I am qualified to be a comedian.
— STEVE MARTIN, "Born Standing Up"

Early that defining Saturday morning in 1965, my dad shocked the world—well, my mom and me, anyway—when he announced that he *wasn't* going to Belmont Park. "Yeah, Marion, I got some schtuff to do and me an the kid are gonna take-a-ride...," he said, hooking his thumb at me. His ever-present stubby White Owl cigar oozed gobs of saliva. "I'll jus drop Stevie off late-uh, then I'm goin' to Yonkers," as in Yonkers Raceway to gamble on the horses. This was part of my dad's usual day-night doubleheader. During the week he'd drive a small box truck delivering all kinds of paper goods in the tri-state area and do his best to finish up by mid-morning. (To this day I still have some of the bright yellow SCHOOL'S OPEN, DRIVE CAREFULLY! plastic bags that fell off that truck.) He'd usually finish his day with an all-night poker game.

How did my mom put up with him for *forty-seven* years?

"Okay, Stevie," he said. "You and me, kid, are gonna take a ride. Get what ya need."

Thanks Pop!

Meanwhile, my mom was busy scribbling down her usual weekend checklist of things to buy in duplicates, triplicates and even quadruplicates to stack in her already overflowing cupboards.

There were seven of us for my mom to keep after: me, my father, my two brothers, Berny and Ira (one became a cop, the other a crook), my sister Judy, and Grandma Rosie, who threw expletives around like a discus champion.

Pass the fuckin' salt.

It's too fuckin' hot in here! Can't ya go to Crazy Eddie's and get a damn blower?

And why's there always shit on the tube?

Like peeling wallpaper, we just got used to Grandma Rosie—well, until company came; then we cringed, especially at the dinner table when people almost choked on their food in shock at Rosie's vernacular. Yes, Mom had her hands full big-time with the Magnificent Seven....

From left to right: Berny, Judy, Aaron, Marion, me and Ira. (Grandma Rosie was off taking diction lessons.)

Long before the days of Costco, Sam's Club, and BJ's made buying in bulk fashionable, my mom was the Queen of the Hoarders. We never had to worry about not having enough Charmin to squeeze or being down to the last drop of Maxwell House Coffee or having enough Bounty paper towels should Niagara Falls suddenly relocate to our cramped apartment on Bronx Boulevard.

My mom had the creative mind of a gambler and she was always one step ahead of my dad in getting money out of him before he ultimately lost it gambling. Often, she would take the food from our refrigerator and bring it across the hall to our neighbor's house, leaving our refrigerator empty. Then before my dad left for the track, she'd tell him to give her money because she had to go food shopping. Of course, he moaned and groaned about how much money he'd already given her, but when she showed him the empty refrigerator, he had no choice.

This was how Mom had the money to turn the lights back on or pay the phone bill when he "forgot" to pay them.

No wonder I'm so smart. (I guess it came from Mom.)

> On days when blizzards blanketed the area and traveling was hazardous to your health, people in our building knew where they could still go food shopping: our house. My mom would hang a sign on our door.
>
> **WE HAVE MILK**

On that fateful July day, mom sensed where my dad was taking me and was about to say something when he spoke first: "Don't worry about it," he said, waving his hand and effectively cutting off any communication on the subject. "Stevie'll be fine."

"I got a surprise for ya, kid," he said, in a raspy, sing-song voice.

I'll take door number three!

He made it sound like Monty Hall but without any choices. To that day I had never given gambling much thought—though I sensed that whenever the subject of this seven-year-old needing a hand-out for, say, a scooter pie at lunch, it was best to ask my mom. I'd soon learn that my dad's wallet was off-limits—unless there was a flip of the cards, a roll of the dice, or a horse to be wagered on.

Actually, having a dad like mine today could be beneficial to a growing youngster, and perfect for learning the alphabet:

A, B, C, D, E, F, G, off we go to OTB.

H, I, J, K, L, M, N, O, P, don't tell your mother you went with me!

My dad started gambling in grade school. He and his little buddies would get together at school recess and use their lunch money and pitch pennies in the school yard. After school, they would meet in the basement of a friend's house in the Bronx and up the ante a bit. Using a worn out Kraft cheese box with three little holes cut out—one for 5¢, 10¢, and 25¢—they'd roll their marbles in their own variation of skee ball; if your glittering marble landed in one of the holes, it was pay up time for the other boys....

From there it was making small bets on baseball games, hanging out in smoke-filled pool halls, being a gofer at a local bookie joint, daily excursions to Aqueduct....

We ended up at the Allerton Avenue Social Club. This was my first look at a "legal" poker room. In the years ahead, I would learn that, in NYC, poker rooms and illegal betting parlors were as commonplace as betting windows at a racetrack. This club, however, was nothing like you'd expect if you were weaned on *The Godfather* trilogy or read the *New York Daily News* or *New York Post*. There was no Vinny 'The Chin' or 'Fat Sally' or Sammy 'The Bull' or anyone with classic literary monikers that hung out there. And there was no wannabe Playboy Bunny with cleavage up the wazoo, either. That was a Bronx Tale, Hollywood at its finest.

Remember the scene in *The Godfather* where
Sonny Corleone gets massacred at the tollbooth?
I was thinking, Sonny Corleone could still be
alive today if he had E-ZPass.

The smoky club was like a frat house for older men. It was a gathering for misguided souls, husbands that were cheating on their wives and stopped by to freshen up a bit, husbands who were *thinking* of cheating on their wives, secret meetings, and money drops. More than anything, though, it was a place to go to chill out and escape from the banalities of life. Plus, win a few bucks at cards or a roll of the dice.

It seemed like there was some type of gambling going on there 24/7, 365. The club was a small series of interconnected rooms with a kitchenette and small island set off by a curtain of beads, which was the "in" thing back in the mid-1960's. The dinette featured a scarred hardwood poker table, each player having their own little slots for things like poker chips, bills, makeshift ashtrays, and stray M & M's (plain or peanut). The tiny living room featured a threadbare couch accompanied by a lamp with a pleated shade, an old Zenith television with rabbit ears encased in aluminum foil, and a massive jukebox that took up an entire wall. How many times did I watch with utter fascination as that mechanical marvel plucked a record out of its slot, deposited it onto a tiny record player in the exposed glass, and watch it spin…and spin…and spin?

I mean, back then I was just a bit too young to gamble, so what else was I supposed to do? Eventually, the novelty of the jukebox wore off and I got sick of hearing the same old songs. There were more geezers in that thing than a nursing home. Crooners like Dean Martin, Perry Como, Bing Crosby, and Frank Sinatra were the only records the jukebox was stocked with.

Yikes!

Seriously, how many times could a sane individual hear Sinatra's "That's Life" or "Strangers in the Night" without going nuts? And now they won't let me forget it: at the end of every Yankee home game, win lose or eliminated from the playoffs, Sinatra's "New York, New York" is played after the final out. (Luckily, beer sales in the stands stop once Kate Smith belts out "God Bless America" in the seventh inning, and I'm on my way home.)

There were so many times we went to the club and my dad said, "Jussit down there for a little while, woncha, Stevie? Hey Delores, get the kidda Coke!" Then he'd shoo me away like a bothersome fly. "C'mon Stevie, just sit over there and...we'll be outta here in a little while." Then he'd go back to his poker hand and flip a bunch of chips into the pot. His buddies used to say, "Stevie, go punch in some songs on the juke." Then they'd turn to my dad. "He's a fine kid, Aaron. Hopefully he won't turn out like you!"

They'd have a good laugh at that.

"Just siddown on the couch and be a good boy, Stevie, and we'll be outta here soon. Promise."

Just how many times did I fall asleep watching television and leave the club with my disgruntled dad long past midnight? How many times did I leave that place with tufts of hair going this way and that and my father silent on the quick ride back though the darkened neighborhood, still smoking that smelly cigar!

A few middle-aged women worked the club and waited on the boys in turn for a meager salary and tips from their poker-playing studs. They made tuna fish sandwiches, wiped up the *O* rings left by a cup of coffee or a can of Coke with a splash of vodka, and answered the phones. Those they answered with deft touches, naturally. *"Louie? No, no...he's not here...I haven't seen him in a while." "Paulie...? I'll ask around for him, but he ain't been here in a few weeks!"* Meanwhile, there was Louie studying his poker hand as if contemplating buying a fine timepiece while Paulie sat over on the couch watching Willis Reed snatch another rebound. Most of the "broads," as my father called them, looked like they'd spent many a night warming themselves on a subway grating.

Now growing up in these environs might seem strange, but I never thought it was much different than how other kids were living—until you're old enough to realize that it wasn't quite "normal." Let's just say my upbringing wasn't quite *Father Knows Best*—it was more like *Leave it to Beaver* meets *The Sopranos*.

Not too hard to predict, but when I got older, I started playing in the poker games at the club, and even against my father. I sometimes won a lot; I sometimes lost a lot; and often I beat my dad out of big pots. (I had my beaten-up Volkswagen Fastback by then so I didn't have to worry about a ride home.) One day, I asked Ralphie, who ran the club, innocently enough, "Hey, how 'bout a little Elvis or the Beatles in the jukebox? I mean, I've been hearing the same shit for years!"

"Lazarus?" he said, pointing at me with dead seriousness. "One more crack like that...and it'll be the last time you ever play here."

Like Frank and Nancy Sinatra, I'd said something stupid.

It was, however, because of my dad's trivial pursuits at the club that we ended up at Old Timers' Day at the Stadium on July 31, 1965 with the Yanks taking on the Cleveland Indians: one of dad's poker-playing buddies didn't have the cash he owed him but offered him a pair of left field seats to the game, instead. My father wasn't happy about that, no sirree Bob, but I guess he figured he could kill two birds with one stone—and never have to listen to me beg him to take me to a game again.

"How many times do you need to actually go to a game?" he'd say later when the subject of a return trip to the Stadium arose. "What's wrong wid watchin' the Yanks on Channel 11?" It would turn out to be the first game, and the last, I'd ever see live with dear old dad.

Shock!
I remember originally thinking that Old-Timers' Day meant that the

older crowd, over fifty I guessed, would get into the Stadium for free. My dad, with his receding Vitalis-styled hair, bushy eyebrows set strongly over his Jack Benny glasses, and Salvador Dali mustache, was forever over fifty.

We made a few "stops" on the way to the game, and each time my dad would tell me, "Be patient, Stevie, we'll get there." (Hmm, looking back, I wonder if the stops had anything to do with gambling . . .) We made it to the Stadium by the fourth inning, but the thrill of that day was overwhelmed by my dad's strange behavior during the game.

We got to the game after Joe DiMaggio hit a homerun in the Old Timers' game; after Joe Pepitone swatted a homerun in the third inning of the regular game (darn!); and only after my father finished complaining about, in no particular order: the damn Stadium traffic, ticket takers, people crowding us in the stands, ushers, Pinkerton guards, and everything short of the state of affairs in Bangladesh.

Ironically, no Stadium vendors ever served us—*You ate already at the club, dincha? How couldja be so hungry already?*—so I never got to try those ballpark franks, those same-style dogs that would be sold for the ungodly sum of five bucks at the turn of the 21st Century. (In hindsight, I probably spared my dad some gambling money on Rolaids.)

What we weren't spared was an unobstructed view of the game! Our outfield seats were behind one of the many huge steel beams that supported the old Yankee Stadium like dental implants.

Can you see them in my program?

But even that didn't bother me so much; I just craned my head when I had to. My "fondest" memory of that strange day has nothing to do with seeing the historic facades that circled the Stadium or the immense electronic scoreboard with the familiar red-white-and-blue Yankee top hat logo that stood out like the Bat Signal. (The scoreboard even blotted out most of the apartment building and Bronx County Courthouse directly behind it.) Nor was it was seeing how the silken grass was cut into perfect diagonal strips or how the fabled monuments sat smack-dab at the base of the centerfield wall . . .

What will stay with me until they lower me into position in my birthday suit as *The Pope and Me* at Yankee Stadium plays Broadway with a Shakespearean-trained thespian in the lead, is this: with the Yanks down two runs late in the game, my man Pepitone smashed one outta the park to tie the score—only to see my dad curse under his breath.

Huh?

At the time I just couldn't understand it and was too confused to ask what was up with that? Didn't he know Pepitone was my hero? Wasn't he thrilled he'd just tied the game? When the game ended with the Yanks eking out a win in the bottom of the ninth, my dad stood silent as the crowd erupted in ecstasy. Then he made like The Flash and dragged me back to the car.

I didn't get it. Didn't he want the Yanks to win? Why wasn't he thrilled when they did? And why was he giving me the silent treatment?

What had I done wrong?

So many times I watched him at home root for Mickey to belt one out of the park or Whitey to strike out the bastard or Tony Kubek to start the backend of a double-play...so why was he so unhappy when the Yanks won that day?

At my age, how was I to know he'd simply bet against them?

> I always knew my dad was a terrible gambler. I mean, who else would bet against the Harlem Globetrotters?

SECOND INNING

Career Opportunities

If you want to make God laugh, tell him about your plans.
— WOODY ALLEN

THERE'S A VENDOR FRIEND of mine who's a tad overweight. Most people would think he was fairly big. If you were camped out next to him at the beach, you'd think Moby Dick had washed ashore.
Thar he blows!
One late January day, my friend asked his wife if she'd consider taking a getaway weekend to an upstate ski lodge to, well, ahem!, rekindle the old flames. (Naturally, this was in that Dead Sports Zone period after the Super Bowl and before the start of Spring Training.) His wife shot back, "Ski lodge? You need an *extra* lodge!" (They never went.) He told me: "You'll see, Steve! I'm gonna start going to the gym and get in shape. Definitely!" Okay, I said. Sure. See you at the ballpark.
When I spoke with him a few weeks later, he claimed he'd been going to the gym just about every day and was working real hard to get in shape. "I think it's working," he said. "Wait'll the guys see me at the Stadium!" (Admittedly, I was hoping he'd have gastric bypass surgery and maybe miss a few months recuperating. He happened to have more seniority than me. Hey if a little stomach stapling would make him look and feel better—and I'd move up a spot in seniority and make a few extra bucks each game—who was I to argue?)
When I saw him on a blustery Opening Day, the dawn of a new Yankee season as palpable as the winds whipping up around the grand old park, he looked like he'd *gained* a few pounds. Swirls of empty beer

cans, fast food wrappers, and discarded coffee cups seemed to be magnetically drawn to him.

I was flabbergasted.

"I know you said you were going to the gym," I told him, "but are you actually going *inside*?" He didn't think I was very funny that day. Such is the life of a comic.

It was sort of like that in college. In 1975, fresh out of Evander Childs High School in the Bronx, a school that served as a "proving ground" for comedians Judd Hirsch *(Taxi)*, Red Buttons and Carl Reiner, I enrolled in Lehman College. I didn't even consider going away to college. After all, how would I gamble at Yonkers or Roosevelt Raceway at night or go to OTB (Off Track Betting) in-between classes? Remember, this was in a day and age before you could do just about everything and anything with the click of a mouse. Lehman was a short bus ride from my house but a world away from where I really wanted to be—as far away from any school as possible. And, besides, outside of Studio 54, the all-the-rage nightclub in the '70s, what better place to meet young, nubile women than in college? So what was an 18-year-old Jew with a nose for numbers—and a Jimmy Durante schnoz to match—with aspirations of being an accountant to do? Stick to the numbers: go to college and the racetrack. After all, hadn't my father supported our family all these years doing double-duty?

After nearly two years at college (and the first Lazarus to even make it to one), the refrain of the brotherhood of the Tau Epsilon Phi fraternity of which I was a member, was: We know you go to Lehman, Steve, but do you actually go *into* the classes?

It was true: I spent more time at the frat house just off the campus on Bainbridge Ave., than I did in school. I did, however, study studiously every day and night—the track programs that is—and by January 1977, I'd accumulated a grand total of nine college credits.

I didn't do very well in college. You see the main problem for me was at the end of the semester, my grade index was two-point one. Unfortunately, my alcohol level was four-oh.

I just couldn't get into the grind and had little interest in my classes. Paleolithic-era professors thumbed through marble composition notebooks with brittle pages droning on and on in cavernous lecture halls, their monotonous voices absorbed by front-row students and acoustic walls. They had little tolerance for any jokes, let alone the ones I'd throw in now and again in an attempt to inject some life into the fossil-like atmosphere. It didn't work, and it was usually met with a hard stare from both professor and student alike. That feeling would resurface in the coming years, sometimes in cavernous banquet halls and sometimes in little hole-in-the-wall bars where shit-faced patrons made me long for those carefree college days of yore.

> That's the true harbinger of spring,
> not crocuses or swallows returning to Capistrano,
> but the sound of a bat on the ball.
> - BILL VEECK

As winter's chill began to thaw and the semblance of actual sidewalks began to appear in my neighborhood, the blackish-grey mounds left by Old Man Winter created dazzling sun-drenched streets, playgrounds alive with children's laughter, and, ultimately, anticipation of a new baseball season just around the corner. (Well, once you hopped on the 4 train).

Newspapers like the *Daily News*, *The New York Times*, and the *New York Post* would soon be filled with Florida Grapefruit League gossip on the comings-and-goings of the New York Yankees and their crosstown rivals New York Mets.

Sure, in the spring a young man's fancy turns to women as they begin to peel their layers of clothing like a ripened banana but—truthfully?—the femme fatale is fertile hunting year-round. You could be locked in a humongous freezer, mounds of beef hides surrounding you like in the Rocky movies and *still* you're thinking of them.

Some things never change.

But baseball in the spring? The first pitch of the Grapefruit League season is akin to divine intervention in the middle of a drive-by.

Back in 1977, amidst an enveloping backdrop of seething violence in the city, the Son of Sam killings, where young couples were hunted like game, a human fly, George Willig, scaling the South Tower of the World Trade Center (for which New York City Mayor Abe Beame would eventually fine him $1.10—or a penny per floor), and a peanut farmer in the White House, I'd come to a crossroads…and had no idea which road to take, nor where any ones might lead in the future.

My yellow brick road was under serious construction.

The realization that school was a complete waste of time became obvious. Back then, college, even a city school like Lehman, wasn't a dozen easy payments of $3995; it was maybe six hundred bucks for the term, tops, and Mother Marion was paying for it—when she was able to separate my father from his gambling stash. As much as I hated to admit it, it was time to get a real job and pack it in at school.

So I did, though of course my parents were the last to know. *Aren't they always?* A friend of mine had a friend of a friend and…you know the deal. It was a job dealing with accounts and ledgers but, mainly, numbers—albeit a distant relative to the accounting position I thought I'd wrangle one day upon graduating. The accommodations weren't great, health benefits were practically non-existent, and the company offered no retirement plan. There weren't many perks other than short hours, no late nights, a relaxed dress code, and you got paid in cash on Fridays. There was optional weekend work and supposedly, if the office had a profitable year, they'd give a nice Christmas bonus. Additionally, I was told some customers could be very generous; bosses, too, on occasion.

My office was equipped with all the little things I'd need for the job: a small desk with a huge mesh cup to hold an army of pens, pencils, and Sharpies, a phone, and my own refrigerator. Eventually I'd have to replace the Borden's Milk crate they'd provided for me to sit on.

There were a couple of pockmarked couches with cigarette burns, a rickety wooden table filled with magazines like *Mad*, *Cracked* and *Newsweek*, as well as old standbys *Playboy* and *Penthouse*. In addition there were the three major dailies and a series of colored sheets with equally colorful names like "Big Red," "The Brooklyn Handle," and "Black Cat Weekly." Customers read them like scripture. Their hope? To hit that day's "New York Number."

Yup, my life was taking a turn for the "bettor." From college life to part of a bookmaking operation, just like that. No experience required.

Hurry! Hurry boys and girls! Come see the transformation before your very eyes! Watch the young Jew join the organized crime rackets and screw up the little life he had!

Here was an opportunity to be a part of the teeming illegal numbers business right here in Da Bronx. Thanks for setting the example, Dad.

"Policy," as it's known in the Penal Code (coined after insurance policies that basically took bets on one's future), or "numbers" as it's known on the street, was big business back then and it's just as big now.

Policy is simply a three digit number. The three digits are determined by adding up the win, place, and show prices for the day at the local racetrack and using the last three numbers to the left of the decimal point. For example, if the total money bet at the racetrack was $1,121,158.40, the number for that day would be "1-5-8." People would bet all kinds of combinations trying to hit this number. Birthdays, anniversaries, numbers people saw in their dreams, their address and phone numbers, the day they filed for bankruptcy, whatever, were inspirations for their bets. The payoffs could range anywhere from 8-1 to 600-1 odds.

Today, New Yorkers are bombarded with legal lottery numbers games offering a staggering array of ways to hit the "jackpot." Proprietors parade glittering signs in display windows and at checkout counters like beauty pageant contestants on a runway.

TONIGHT'S LOTTO JACKPOT IS $35.3 MILLION!
What are you waiting for?

There are hologram-like tickets offering the wondrous vistas of the New York skyline to the brilliance of the shimmering Niagara Falls to bucolic settings where little bunny rabbits share nature with picnickers laying out a checkered tablecloth in a secluded area of a state park—all in an effort to fill state coffers from a form of entertainment once relegated to back rooms.

There are jackpots and scratch-offs and daily drawings, oh my!

Lotto, Mega Millions, Take Five, Win 4, Quick Draw, Pick 10, Deal or *No Deal*, *Big Buck$*, *Ca$htastic*, *White Ice*, *Cash Frenzy*, and *New York Millions*. There are a slew of scratch-off lottery tickets with alliterative names for the closet poet like *Raffle to Riches*, *Big Buck*, and *Bada Bling*.

There are *Mega Millions* and *Powerball* lotteries nationwide and enough gamblers who have a "Dollar and a Dream" to come back again and again in their efforts to live the high life and escape the clutches of domesticity.

Looking for a neat Valentine's gift for that female in your life? You can pick out your very own star from the International Star Registry for a mere $49.95 ("Look, honey, it comes with its very own Certificate of Authenticity!"), or if that's too much, then how about *Hearts are Wild*, the newest instant scratch-and-win game from the New York Lottery? Are we that far from a sniff-and-smell lotto? *Your nose knows how to pick a winner!* HAVE YOU SNIFFED AND SMELLED TODAY?

When I started taking numbers, just down the street from the Burke Avenue Unemployment Office, there was a limited amount of lottery games and most people pooh-poohed the idea—thinking it was a sucker's game and one that honest, respectable citizens didn't play, no matter how many state officials said the proceeds were targeted towards education. Now, lotteries are an accepted form of gambling and a quick fix for many ills. Some lottery tickets come in rolls and are literally dispensed like toilet paper at your local candy store. And despite all the legislators that look to make a name for themselves by shutting down a bookmaker's operation around Super Bowl time, despite all the talk that sports is being ruined by all the game-day betting lines and that certain types of gambling is akin to warts on a super model, have you noticed the proliferation of lottery games, billion-dollar casinos, and celebrity-fueled poker tournaments?

Now you can even purchase a lottery numbers *subscription*!

There are so many scratch-off lottery games today:
Win five-hundred a week for life, win a thousand a week for life,
and now they even have a special one when you're down
to your last buck: *Take my Life, Please.*

In the illegal numbers and bookmaking racket, there are betting parlors set up all over the country, but especially in the inner cities. Indeed, every neighborhood has one. They're not too tough to spot: just look for the faded Mattel toy robot in the grimy, sun-faded plate-glass window or inside a dilapidated storefront where on a lone shelf you're apt to find Aunt Jemima sharing space with Uncle Ben and Minute Maid Rice - and nothing else. They're in the back rooms of pizza shops, delicatessens, dry cleaners, flower shops, in the back of auto parts stores adorned with barely clad calendar girls clinging to fuzzy dice-laden Hot Rods, and behind sequined curtains at Chinese restaurants. Sometimes, the places are just *places*, like mine was back in the day.

Happily, for those who want to bet on credit, for those that don't want to wait in line as people fumble for their list of numbers based on their children's birthdays or the anniversary of the day they lost their virginity in the back seat of a '49 Ford, for those that don't want to wait as old folks straighten out crumpled wads of bills or scour their purse for their five-dollar winning lotto ticket so they can exchange it for another five-dollars worth of tickets, there's still the sanctum of the back room at the neighborhood tavern. Alas, the illegal numbers trade still thrives in New York like a cabbie in search of a fare.

I was watching the lottery drawings the other day on TV. They said the regular lottery lady, Yolanda Vega, who calls out the numbers, was on vacation. What does that mean she's "on vacation?" What does she work, 15 seconds a night? What's that, two hours a year? How is she *on vacation*? I'd like to be a fly on the wall at her next job interview when the interviewer looks at her resume and says, *Wow, you pull balls! We'll see you Monday morning at nine!*

Having grown up in the environs, it seemed only natural that I would gravitate to the business. My dad, who'd set up a bookmaking operation in our *house* shortly after, would be one of the few bookmakers to actually lose money, and be out of business not long after he started. At the end of every week, I collected money from the losers and paid off the winners. Ironically, this was the way I'd end up getting

YOLANDA VEGA

my job at Yankee Stadium.

Once I got the job, I almost lost it just as quick thanks to Dear Old Dad.

* * *

After about three months of sitting on that Borden's milk crate, I was not only taking bets on numbers but wagers of all kinds: horse racing, college and pro sports, and even exhibition games and golf tournaments. (Today you can even bet on individual quarters of a football game, the opening coin toss, or on a presidential election—all from the comfort of your own home!) Bettors were offered a smorgasbord of possibilities: basketball, hockey, baseball, pre-season and post-season games, you name it. Had the Dead Pool - where you pick the celebrity who will croak first - been alive and well back then, I'm sure we would've taken action on that, too.

Every once in a while my friends in the business (birds of a feather flock together) would get "inside information."

"I'm tellin' ya, Steve," they'd say. "Dis horse can't lose!" Sometimes the tips would pan out. Most often, however, they'd fizzle out like a shaken soda can.

In short order, I'd gotten used to the life. Gotten used to schmoozing with customers, taking wagers on little yellow carbon-copy slips with bets for that day's Brooklyn Number or individual daily numbers, gotten used to watching sporting events with an eye on the bottom line, gotten used to no school and few hassles. And the money was good. It was, as Tony Bennett, sang so often on that darn juke, "The Good Life."

Until I got a tip that would change me forever. Well, for a short time, anyway.

"The police are coming," my friend said over the phone, "and you'd better get the *fuck* outta there." The movie version of *The Pope and Me at Yankee Stadium* might show a long black phone cord draped over the desk with the receiver hanging limp inches from the floor and the tabletop radio in the background tuned to WINS 1010 News radio reporting another Son of Sam bloodbath in the city. *Are ya still there, Steve?* Customers being urged to leave quickly as a pile of evidence is stuffed into a big black bag by the frenzied numbers-taker...but having been briefed that there was always an "outside chance" of being arrested—"They only bother ya once-in-a-while outside Manhattan," I was told, "and they don't usually bother ya in the Bronx"—I always had it in the back of my mind that there was an outside chance that I'd be "pinched."

I'd heard the stories from my friends who said jail wasn't none too fun, even short stints. Once in a while, some of them had to suffer a seventy-two hour weekend stay if they happened to be busted on a Friday. (Hey, judges can't make golf dates during the week.)

In the real-life version of *The Pope and Me*, I methodically packed up the betting slips, wrapped a White Owl cigar box with a couple of rubber bands so no bills or coins would spill out and scrammed!

Just the thought of even a smidgeon of jail time was enough to scare me. How often had I heard my brother, Berny the Cop, talk of all the people he'd arrested, the flotsam and jetsam that he had to deal with on a daily basis as a plainclothes detective in the Fordham section of the Bronx, and the deplorable conditions of city jails?

Whether it was a winning tip and the cops came or not, I'll never know, but my days as a policy maker were over. No job was worth going to jail for, at least not for this scaredy cat.

* * *

Not long after, I made a big money drop for my father to a pudgy, bearded man with jowls that hung like saddlebags. He was in a damn fine mood, yes indeed, as I handed him his hefty winnings. In turn, he told me that he worked at Yankee Stadium and was in charge of the vendors. I never did understand why I hadn't gone to the Stadium earlier to get a job, but I recognized a career opportunity when I was offered a job right then and there.

And lo and behold, at the age of 19, I'd gotten my first real job. In the next 20 years, I'd have a myriad of jobs including golf caddy, short-order cook, plant store caretaker, assistant manager at McDonalds, part-owner of a six-lane bowling alley (including Lane 5 and the men's bathroom), and the requisite accounting jobs...though I always remained partial to my job as a Yankee Stadium vendor. It was *the* job—until I got the nerve to give comedy a shot. Before that, anything that involved less than carrying a metal tray with two-dozen cans of beer up and down an aisle had little appeal to me.

After all, I found that often 9-to-5 jobs—*way too often*—got in the way of a good tan. How many times would I have to leave my job at 11:00 a.m. so I'd get a good spot at my pool club to work on my tan? I knew that pretty soon I'd put an end to that nonsense.

THIRD INNING

The 48th Major League Baseball
All-Star Game—the start of my dual career
July 19, 1977

*You should enter a ballpark the
way you enter a church.*

- BILL LEE

"NO PROBLEM GETTING YOU a job," the pudgy man with the saddlebags under his eyes, said. "If you want one." He counted out the money I gave him from his week's winnings, his grubby little paws fingering each bill methodically, smoothly. "Come by the Stadium and I'll hook you up."

"*Seriously?*"

I'd been a regular at Yankee games most of my life, attending 15-20 games a year, so for me this was a dream come true, the job I'd wanted since I was that young whippersnapper in grade school. I always thought it was worth it just to see the games, and now I was going to get paid as well.

Even now people tell me, "Wow! You get to see all the games! Cool." Of course, they always add, "Hey, have you ever met Derek Jeter?"

"Sure," I say. "We go to Hooters after every Yankee game."

"Really?"

I always figured you had to have some connection to get in, sort of like knowing the Asian lady in the nail salon for a free back wax. How ironic was it that right around that time, local papers were actually advertising for vendors because the annual Major League Baseball All-Star Game was at the Stadium?

I was about to become a regular on my own Fantasy Island.

De plane, boss, de plane!

The Beer Man cometh.

– – –

Litell delivers ... High drive to right-center field...
It could be...it is...gone! Chris Chambliss has won the American League pennant for the New York Yankees...A thrilling, dramatic game ...What a way for the American league season to end!
- KEITH JACKSON + HOWARD COSELL, ABC-TV

– – –

Before being swept by the Big Red Machine in the 1976 World Series, Chris Chambliss left an indelible impression in the hearts and minds of all Yankee fans—including one future Beer Man—with his homerun that just cleared the 353 FT. sign in right-center field.

Who can forget the television shot of #10 exulting after the ball sailed over the wall giving the Bombers their first pennant since 1964? Who could forget Chambliss' desperate trip around the bases clutching his helmet as pandemonium erupted and a swarm of delirious fans streamed onto the field attempting to mob him? Who could forget the fans clawing, pulling, jerking, tripping, ripping, gripping, tearing, lunging, and falling over one another trying to get a piece of him? Or the images of Chambliss tripping over fans and then making like Franco Harris in twisting and turning and tucking away his helmet like a football player in search of the goal line, dodging the loonies and steamrolling and sideswiping and forearming and bowling them over en route to the sanctity of the clubhouse and escape from the clutches of the Bronx Zoo?

Who could forget those upper deck shots as a frenzied mass of humanity acted like renegade ants discovered under a picnic rock as the Stadium scoreboard flashed WE'RE #1 WE'RE #1 WE'RE #1?

Funny, but that bedlam was what I thought of when I walked out into the upper deck behind home plate for my first game as a Yankee Stadium vendor on July 19, 1977. I was an employee of Canteen Corporation (later to be renamed Centerplate), and I was "King of the World."

Over thirty years later, I still feel that way. Well, just about.

* * *

I'm often reminded of the classic Norman Rockwell-painted Saturday Evening Post cover with the Red Sox rookie (yes, I know, Buck Foston!) on the cover. My debut at the Stadium as a rookie was one impossible to forget. I was that kid in the clubhouse that knew no one, had no clue as to where anything was, and though I made eye contact with many of the vendors, I seemed to sense that I posed a "threat" to many of them. It was soon obvious that it this was a common thread that rookies faced not only in stadiums and ballparks but in any place where commission vending exists, then and now; from here to eternity. Like in real estate, it was all about location, location, location, and watch where you go and what territory you tread upon. In other words, *Don't vend in my area, dude!*

And make sure you follow the vending rules, rules that have been around—and in all likelihood haven't changed a whole darn lot—since Ruth and Gehrig and Co. made the Concourse Plaza Hotel at 161 St. the place to wine, dine and bed down for the evening.

Company rules like:

- Dishonesty with merchandise or money, or any attempt to defraud a customer will not be tolerated. If found in violation you will be subject to termination. *You mean we're supposed to give back change? Even to little kids and immigrants?*
- No one is permitted to bring friends or relatives into the ballpark. If found, you will be subject to termination. *If you fire me, can I at least*

finish watching the game?
- Discourtesy to our customers is STRICTLY prohibited. Under NO CIRCUMSTANCES will employees be permitted to engage in an argument with any patron. If a problem should arise, call a supervisor immediately. *Am I allowed to wipe off the spit from the fan—or do I have to get security clearance first?*
- Reporting for duty while under the use of alcohol or any intoxicating substance, or the use of any substance while on the premises will subject you to termination. *Aww, that's not fair! You let Doc Gooden and Daryl Strawberry and Roger Clemens and Jason Giambi work, so why can't I? How else do you expect me to run around for three straight hours carrying a forty pound case of beer?*
- Obscene language is not to be used while in the building. Employees using obscene language will be sent home and/or disciplinary actions will be taken. *That's bullshit and I, for one, won't fucking stand for that!*
- We expect our employees to be well groomed and neatly dressed AT ALL TIMES. The company does have the right to send an employee home if their attire does not meet company standards. *I think that's ridiculous that I can't wear my custom-designed New York Yankees nose ring!*

Good evening, Mr. Lazarus, vendor #2711. Your mission, should you decide to accept, is sell refreshing Pepsi Cola to as many fans as you can. And make sure you give back the change!

"Hey, I gave you twenty bucks and you only gave me back change for a ten."
"Sorry, you'll have to see Mr. Steinbrenner at the end of the game after he's checked the register."

That first night was anything but an All-Star one. After obviously being thrilled to be here—*imagine, me working at Yankee Stadium, oh boy!* — the joy was tempered somewhat by the daunting physical task.

A place where so much history had been made, I thought, and here I was about to make my own: being the first vendor to work one game and quit. (I was later to learn that there was once a vendor who sold a couple of trays of soda, kept the proceeds, and simply walked off into the wild blue yonder.)

I never even stayed for the end of the All-Star game, which was won by the National League: I was simply too pooped. *Once is quite enough*, I remember thinking; *I'm not cut out for this*! Having to scale the death-defying steps of the Mt. Everest-like upper deck while balancing a heavy tray of soda in my hands, was enough to convince me that maybe I should have left well enough alone, relegated myself to listening to the radio or TV for future Yankee games. The money I made, about fifty-two bucks in commission, was awesome for around three hours work, especially since minimum wage was a little over two bucks an hour in '77. I came home and collapsed in my bed and told my mom "Never again!" Just the mere thought of trying to make it up those daunting steps was enough to keep me away.

But somehow I returned. I can't tell you if it was my mom who said give it another shot or my dad who pushed me to go back (possibly thinking that somewhere down the road he may need to borrow a few bucks from me)...but we humans sometimes have short memories—and for want of a quick buck tend to put up with some things that others might not. So I lived to fight another day. Plus I'd developed this little gambling habit, and I could sure use the cash.

Now, it's a struggle to get out of bed, my body ravaged from climbing too many of those Yankee Stadium steps selling anything from cotton candy to knishes to peanuts to popcorn, ice cream, hot dogs and, of course, brewskis. I've banged into too many railings, been scalded by countless sterno-fueled hot dog bins, and lugged too many cases of beer filled with enough ice to sink the Titanic. Even my pre-game rituals are tiring, which I'll tell you about later. (*The Pope and Me* documentary will show actual footage of my battered and scarred but still sexy body.)

It's a living, though. Vending is in my blood, so I go on and on and on . . . and here I am three decades later still standing - and still vending. Along with a number of other hearty "old-timers," I'm still running my ass off, still dodging errant line drives and overzealous fans in the box seats, and still doling out the cold ones and the snappy one-liners.

All this and dealing with the ridiculous rules, too.

And, as Maxwell Smart, Secret Agent 86, said, *loving it*!

I've been vending at the Stadium for over three decades and it's nearly impossible to move up in seniority. I'm vendor #50. Vendor #1 is 86 years-old. He's survived two heart attacks, diabetes, and a gunshot wound—from vendor #2. He was suspended last year when he tested positive for Maalox.

I was there when *Reg-gie! Reg-gie! Reg-gie!* hit three homeruns in Game 6 of the '77 World Series and the following year when Opening Day fans threw their "Reggie Bar" giveaways onto the field following a moonshot by the slugger.

I was there on August 3, 1979, the day after Yankee Captain Thurman Munson died in a plane crash; I can still remember the eerie sight of the pre-game ceremonies in which the Yankees took the field in their defensive positions, except for the catcher's spot. We vended in hushed tones for a good part of the night.

I worked the infamous Pine Tar Game in 1983 when George Brett went ballistic after his homeroom was disallowed (TAR WARS! blared the next day's *New York Post* headline); watched as one-armed pitcher Jim Abbott hurled a no hitter in 1993 and was lucky enough to work perfect games by the two Davids, Wells in 1998 and Cone in '99. I saw the culmination of many of the Yanks' championships during their go-go years.

I was also there during the lean years of the 1980's and early 1990's when the Yankees failed to make the playoffs and you couldn't draw people to the park without some kind of giveaway day like Bat Day, Ball Day or Cap Day. With the Yankees now selling out every game, things have certainly changed.

Four hot dogs, four beers, four souvenir shirts,
four bags of peanuts and four ice creams
all for just four easy payments of $44.95.

During those lean times, with little seniority, and few fannies in the seats, I sold cotton candy on a rainy day (which turns to Kool Aid just like that) or peanuts or soda most of the time. Senior vendors sold dirty-water hot dogs and beer with lids that never quite stayed on. By the time the fans got their suds, it was a miracle if it was still full—or cold! What's incredible is that even today there are simply no lids for beer or coffee or hot chocolate when fans buy them at the counter. It's hilarious (though sad, really) to watch fans make like Philip Petit walk across a taut high wire as he did so famously back in 1974 between the Twin Towers. I can't tell you how many times fans have returned to their seats with nearly empty cups. And what would management's answer be to why there are no lids?

"Well, they would cost a penny a piece and that would drastically cut into our 1000% up on most of our beverages . . ."

So yes, it was frustrating back in the lean years for both fans and struggling vendors alike—and often not much fun making barely enough meal money.

Those were the days before the most recent Yankee dynasty of the late 20th- early 21st century; those were the days when Yankees owner George Steinbrenner threatened to uproot the Yankees from the Bronx that was burning to the safety and sanctity of the West Side of Manhattan or the relatively new and cleaned-up confines of the former swamps of the Meadowlands in New Jersey. Steinbrenner's assertion that fans wouldn't attend because they were too worried about their safety, the headaches that came from the traffic snarls in the area coming and going, and—*can we talk here?*—not enough luxury boxes were just three of the gazillion reasons why he couldn't make it in (this part of) New York. This was before the Yankees started putting notches on their championship belt like a gunslinger picking off ducks in a penny arcade. Suddenly, the South Bronx seemed like a "perfect fit" for the Yankees once again, right across the street from where in 1923 ten acres of undeveloped swampland would soon become the birthplace of the most famous sports stadium in the world.

Amazing what a winning team will do to spruce up a neighborhood, huh? (And how bold fans would become to venture out and see a winner!)

So, yes, I was there in 1996 when Wade Boggs took the most famous ride on a horse since Paul Revere following the Bombers' first World Championship in 18 years amidst the roar of delirious Yankee fans. One of my vendor friends, Allan Gold, who's been here since the 1960's and actually remembers fans exiting the game via the playing field, watched the closing moments holding hands with fellow vendor—and daughter —Alicia and recalls that when third baseman Charlie Hayes caught a pop-up straddling the third base stands for the last out of the 1996 World Series and "squeezed his glove, we both just started crying." As probably did countless Yankees fans around the country, especially when they saw Boggs hitch that ride on a NYPD horse and strode around the Stadium like a conquering hero, dancing and prancing his way into the hearts of New Yorkers for eternity.

Me?

I was down the right field line behind the 318FT. sign, peering in through a plexiglas barrier, surrounded by empty kegs of beer, mountains of garbage, crushed and laced boxes piled a mile high looking for all the world like a junkyard of crushed cars held tight by scads of cellophane wrapping, making for a picturesque display of Yankee paraphernalia near the big Green Monster: the trash compactor. Oh no no no, I couldn't watch the game in the stands with the paying fans. No way, Jose. That's against company policy.

<u>GENERAL WORK RULE #20</u>
All employees must leave the Stadium immediately after their work shift is over. Any employee found congregating in any part of the Stadium is subject to immediate termination.

Hey, I'm supposed to wait here for Derek Jeter. We're going to Hooters!

Puddles of leaking beer, soda, and water accentuated the scene as the Yankees once again were riding high. My view was fit for a vendor and I paid only obligatory notice towards it as I'd gotten—shall we say—used to the panorama, having to dress in the "luxury" of the vendor's locker room. (Stay tuned for all the gory details.)

I was there when Roger Clemens went nuts trying to hit the Mets' Mike Piazza with a jagged barrel of a broken bat handle and I don't recall ever missing a game of the greatest rivalry—and spectacle—in sports: Yankees vs. Red Sox.

I've worked the annual Old-Timers' Day since I started and somehow I can't help looking "forward to" the end of the ceremonies when they give a roll call of who met their maker in the last year. Yeah, it's kind of morbid but I have a strong feeling I'm not alone in this. *I wonder?* Would they mention *my name* one day when they gave the roll call of those that passed away in the last year?

Good! Lazarus is dead—I finally move up a spot in seniority!

* * *

I was in the Stadium when George W. Bush made a surprise appearance that lifted the Stadium's spirits—and a nation's—as he threw out the first ball for Game 3 of the 2001 World Series following the horrors of

9/11. A vendor's rumor had it that the President was disguised as an umpire until moments before he walked on the field.

"I swear," said the vendor requesting anonymity, lest the CIA get word. "He had this giant chest protector on and a face guard and those big pockets umpires have where they keep their balls in…"

I got goose bumps as I balanced on a box seat along with the other Stadium rubberneckers, everyone straining for a better view. President Bush wound up and delivered a perfect strike to the catcher amidst a huge roar. (It was probably the last time he got any kind of cheer.) The appreciative crowd was truly thankful for his effort and inspiration. Not as thankful as I was later that day when I put my beer bin down and found one Benjamin Franklin staring up at me. I looked at that hundred dollar bill - first shocked, then warily - as I deftly put my shoe over it and awaited the moment when it would be yanked from me, the old schoolyard practical joke with the string tied to the bill . . . but it wasn't!

Finders keepers!

Memories, like the corners of my mind....

Interestingly, one of my most vivid memories of my vending career at the Stadium had little to do with what took place on the field, or serving such celebrities as Spike Lee, Tom Hanks, Madonna, Robin Williams, Billy Joel, and Tom Cruise.

During batting practice one day, I was sitting in the left field stands just shooting the bull with my fellow vendors. *How many beers did you do last night? Was the beer cold? What time didja check out? Is your sister still single?* As usual, a bunch of fans were camped out in the area, many in full Yankee regalia, a bunch with their baseball gloves, and all with hopes of catching a souvenir ball.

Look Ethyl! Look what I got at the game today! A real baseball!
Great, Harry. Did ya pay the cable bill yet?

And then there was the fan with the baby …

The batting practice ball banged off one of the metal railings at the bottom of the aisle and ricocheted off a couple of seats when from out of nowhere this thirty-something with khaki jeans, starched shirt, and perfectly coiffed hair (he probably had a Rolex but I didn't take note) lunged for it, diving headfirst right into a pile of human flesh with his baby in his arms!

Like me, many of the vendors that start hawking at the ballpark do so because they're sports fans and it's a perk to get free front-row seats and watch history unfold game after game. Here's our chance to download memories into virtual scrapbooks, some as clear as digital prints.

This surreal scene was an added "bonus."

I still remember the befuddled look that guy had when he realized what he'd done as he emerged unscathed with his bundle of joy: his momentary agony of thinking he'd just crushed his baby - only to find her coo-cooing softly as if her mother had just rocked her gently a few times. Now if you can just imagine a guy behind One Man and a Baby giving a high-five to his friend who caught the prized ball, you'll get a really good picture of the action.

I remember the time my ten-year-old nephew, Ian, a huge Yankee fan, went to his first game in the summer of 1986, and so does he. That was a time before every Stadium worker was subjected to search and seizure. *I'm sorry, sir, you can't bring in that toiletry bag. How do I know that Ban Roll-On isn't a plastic explosive?*

Ian just walked in with me through the employee's entrance.

I changed quickly into my vendor's uniform and we went into the left field stands while the players were out on the warning track doing calisthenics, running laps, and shagging batting practice balls. The usual crowded assortment of loonies were stationed in the lower boxes, awaiting that precious precision-stitched Rawlings baseball hit by some unknown batting practice ballplayer, a five-ounce piece of cowhide that they could one day proudly display on their mantelpiece alongside their pop's ashes.

Suddenly a screeching liner made its way towards us. In unison everyone looked up, tracking the arc of the ball.

Ian, like the father with the baby, his eyes now as big as baseballs, braced himself. *"Uncle Stevie! Uncle Stevie! It's coming this way! Uncle Stevie..."*

And just like that, it caromed off a chair and went right into my hand. My nephew looked at me as if his dream came true. *"You got it Uncle Stevie! You got it!"*

GENERAL WORK RULE #11
*...After the gate opening, any baseballs hit
into the stands are for fans ONLY.*

Without a moment's hesitation I wound up and threw the ball right back onto the field. I had no choice being in my vendor's uniform. The ball took a couple of weak bounces along the foul line.

My nephew's befuddled, puppy dog face told the story. The bootleg copy of *The Pope and Me at Yankee Stadium* up for sale on eBay would show Ian's face sheet-white, as if Dracula had found happiness in the South Bronx.

"How could you?" Ian's look said.

"I like my job," I simply told him, shrugging my shoulders. Then we went to get something to eat. But Ian wasn't hungry.

FOURTH INNING

...Live from New York, it's Saturday Night!
March 4, 1995

Yes, it's tough,
but not as tough as doing comedy.

- EDMUND GLENN, when asked about facing death

I WAS DOOMED.

It was nearly 8:00 p.m., and I was in a panic.

Where the heck were Mark and Mindy?

At the front table of the small piano bar, two wooden folding chairs remained unoccupied, as barren as a desert plain. The overhead fluorescents cast a weak shadow over them. Just ahead, they bathed the wooden stage in an artificial glow, flickers of light bouncing off the baby grand.

It was my stand-up comedy debut at Don't Tell Mama's before a sold-out house, and I was next.

Um, Mr. DeMille, I'm not quite ready for my close-up.

Where were they?

Were they having trouble finding a parking spot in the congested city? Were they stuck in the Lincoln Tunnel like the characters in Stephen King's *The Stand*, civilization on the verge of extinction after a virus epidemic and the tunnel clogged with cars and corpses? Maybe they just couldn't find the place amongst the million other joints along Restaurant Row?

Was that it?

Howling laughter, which once filled the cabaret, had dissipated as the sixth of twelve comedians finished up a tough set. Off to the side, I scanned the back of the room past double rows of tables filled with friends and neighbors and strangers full of wine and drink and half-eaten burgers and fries, for any visible signs of a pair of up-and-coming yuppies entering. I clutched the stage curtain in panic and I was reminded of my first day of nursery school when my mom had to pry my rigid hands from hers in an effort to get me on the school bus. "You'll be fine, Stevie, you'll be okay," she assured me. "Just get on the bus…please? For Mommy? I promise you'll be okay…" But my mom wasn't here now, having died in 1990. I was totally alone now, seconds from my debut, my official entry into the world of stand-up comedy, my chance to leave my imprint on this kind, cruel world, my chance for fame and fortune—or possibly utter humiliation.

And no one was here now to reassure me of anything.

* * *

The comedy class that would serve as my springboard—or would it be a diving board into an empty pool?—was held in a decrepit lower east side tenement in the shadows of the FDR drive. A foreboding cardboard sign affixed to the patchwork lobby door welcomed us:

COMEDY CLASS STUDENTS: TAKE ELEVATOR TO
THIRD FLOOR BUT <u>DO NOT</u> RIDE ALONE!

Three nervous hopefuls rode up in a rickety old-style elevator with a yellowed globe sending splinters of light into the visible shaft around us. None of us looked at each other as we settled in and felt the elevator sink a notch. It was as if we established eye contact in the cramped confines of this crazy contraption, we'd be acknowledging the absurdity of what lay ahead. In order to move the elevator, I had to close a pair of heavy latticed copper and brass gates and maneuver a lever like an old ship's wheel to go up. In doing so, I felt like I was steering a bucking bronco out of the gate.

As we ascended with a jolt, one of the comedy babes shot a glance at me as if to say, *Can you steer this fucking thing or what?*

"Hey, where's the bellboy to take our stuff?" I said with a palpable sigh of relief upon reaching the third floor landing with a clanging. There was no further reaction from Ms. Comedy Babe 1995, a pert little number with nice dangling modifiers that I wouldn't mind trying a little wordplay with after class. (Hopefully, in the film version of *The Pope and Me at Yankee Stadium* the producers would have me sleeping with her.) After a rough start, we'd made it—albeit just a few inches short of ground zero. (It was a fitting start to my comedy career.) We all stepped up and out into the dingy corridor that was reminiscent of the first time I'd visited a West Farms bordello in the Bronx for my sixteenth birthday. All that was missing was the "Oooh baby!" and "Oh yeah honey!" and "I think this is it!" and other assorted moans and groans from behind closed doors. In truth, the atmosphere would be better than some of the dives I'd eventually work at.

Suddenly, my calm and cool vital signs changed to DANGER! SLIPPERY WHEN WET! After all these years of saying that this is what I wanted to do, it dawned on me that here I was actually doing it—and I didn't want to anymore! I just didn't think I could go through with it, and I stopped dead in my tracks, the comedy babe stepping around me.

"You okay?" she said.

"I'm fine," I lied.

You could've probably played connect-a-dot with my beads of sweat as I heard the controlled murmuring down the hall from people that I would *guess* thought they were pretty funny, just like me. And funny enough to eventually give it a try for real. Were they a bundle of nerves too?

With all the things I'd done in my life and all the things I'd put up with, this would be one of the few times when I felt more than butterflies swirling in my stomach, but something twisting it as well. Even when I stupidly got involved with my brother Ira, returning stolen items with a story that I got them for my engagement party, I never felt this nervous. The time when I missed a thousand dollar payment to a bookmaker and he threatened to come after me and break my legs? Nope, not as nervous.

Going into a comedy class where I would eventually have to not only talk in front of total strangers but tell them jokes and make them laugh, well, no way could I do that! After all, strange as it might seem, though

I badly wanted to do this all my life, I had a major fear of standing up in front of total strangers. (Indeed, the No. 1 fear of most people, according to the "Book of Lists," is public speaking, even ranking ahead of the fear of death or listening to my comedy CD.)

When I first had an inkling about taking the comedy class, having read about it in *The New York Times* only weeks before, most of my friends said there was no way I was going to do it. (Sorry, they weren't *smart* enough to use reverse psychology.) Though I had been saying for years that I wanted to do stand-up, I'd never known that classes like this existed. Deep down, my becoming a stand-up comic was, in truth, probably a pipe dream. For years I watched comedians like the late George Carlin, Robert Klein, Bill Cosby, Don Rickles, Joan Rivers, Soupy Sales and Johnny Carson and never for a second did I believe that I could be anything like them. *How could I ever be as good as these guys?*

I always imagined, though, what it must be like to have people laughing at what you said. Not just a casual or witty remark or something funny in the middle of a conversation, but how cool it would be for someone to come to a club expressly to see *me* perform. Growing up (and, okay, even now) there are times I'll lay awake at night, a girl asleep on each arm, and envision Carnegie Hall packed to the rafters with **"Lazarus Rising"** fans as HBO cameras tracked my every move while their mics recorded history. (Hopefully, that botched nose job I had back in '82 wouldn't look too bad on HDTV!)

For weeks I mulled over the idea of taking that comedy class as if contemplating having a life-saving operation.

Now, after having a small "breakdown" outside the elevator on the way to my first comedy class, I got up.

Life-saving operations for two-hundred, Alex.

I entered a room that seemed like it had at one time been a private dick's office with a wannabe Sam Spade taking up residence awaiting a big case to solve. A thin wooden door, topped with cracked opaque glass with peeling black script, opened into a garish green room that was highlighted by a roll top desk in one corner and three rows of metal folding chairs in the middle. That was it. No stage, no bank of overhead lights, no sound system; just a damn broomstick that would serve as a microphone. "And don't mess it up!" said the building's janitor.

It didn't bother me in the least; I'd arrived at my life's destination—and thought I'd shit my pants.

Only later on did I realize that the only interest the proprietor of this "school" had was in making a quick buck. Welcome to New Yawk, buddy, have a nice day and don't let the door hit ya on the way out. Regardless, I had reached my destiny. For the zealous sports fan, this would be their team's trip to the World Series after years of hovering near the cellar; to me, after thirty-eight years in limbo, this was to be the second step in realizing the double-play combo of my dreams.

"*Our friend Lazarus has fallen asleep*," Jesus said, "*but I am going there to wake him up.*" After that, Jesus might've added: "*Let the bum try comedy! What's he gonna do, be a vendor at Yankee Stadium all his miserable life?*"

In a space the size of a large self-storage facility, thirty aspiring comedians didn't seem to care at all about the shape, size, layout or lack of accoutrements. We were going to get it on and do comedy. How could it get any better than that? As I talked to a few people that had paid $350 for four two-hour sessions, a private meeting, and a live appearance at either Caroline's or Don't Tell Mama's in midtown, I calmed down a bit. When our teacher, a Truman Capote look-alike, walked in with a battered briefcase in one hand and a yellow egg timer in the other and announced that each of us would have five minutes to present our material that evening, I stared at him in disbelief. I hadn't even settled into my seat.

"You m-mean we're going to present tonight?" I asked.

"That's right," he said. "You'll be fine."

I looked at the folder of jokes that I'd brought with me, the one that had taken me twenty years to put together, and I collapsed into my chair. I felt sick again.

*   *   *

This comedy class was my chance to talk about my observations, pet peeves, wonderings and wanderings, my view of the world, my take on the ludicrousness of life and people and just about anything under the sun or in our solar system…and with a rapt audience that wanted to be entertained.

I ask ya: is being a comedian really work? How many times had I walked into the accounting firm of Schultheis & Panettieri and come in frumpy and grumpy, having simmered and stewed in traffic on the LIE for an hour, only to find ledgers piled high on my desk...
CALL LEO WASSERMAN THIS AFTERNOON.
DON'T FORGET THE MURPHY ACCOUNT!
THERE'S A BRICKLAYER'S MEETING THIS FRIDAY.
STEVE, I GOT YOU THE SUNTAN LOTION FROM WALGREEN'S.

...and go through them with the interest of a night watchman begrudgingly making his rounds, his motions robotic, his mind numb, his future as secure as his rickety desk chair. How often would I contemplate the rest of the day only to watch the wall clock move with debilitating slowness? I know that for some people just working their 9–5 job is total torture. For me, just working from 9-to-5 minutes after was hell! (So the chance to work maybe a half-hour tops a night as a comic was right down my alley.)

Writing down my thoughts, my observations of multi-million-dollar athletes that went on strike, well, didn't I talk about that with my friends anyway? Talking about my own dating problems, dealing with females or dealing with my dad and the rest of the Lazarus clan or the emotional problems of my friends, this was work? Tellling a joke about going to McDonalds and ordering a meal "to stay" and then being told by the cashier there were no more trays so here's your food in a bag "to go"—even though I can see a mountain of trays off to the side of the Rastafarian with the exploding hair net? That was hard? That was torture? It seemed that everywhere I went, everything I watched, everything I read, and everyone I spoke with was potential fodder for my act. I knew my days as an accountant would soon be "numbered"—and I'd soon learn that using puns in comedy—unless incredibly clever—was one of the worst things you could do.

I couldn't imagine all the comedians that I watched not ever wanting to be on stage forever. I'd gotten a taste of what it felt like to get a laugh just in that dinky room and it was starting to grow on me. There was something about basking in the glow of the spotlight, all eyes on you, the audience at your mercy, here to laugh, to be entertained, and for me to be entertaining them. This was for me. *Kill the fatted calf tonight! Lazarus is alive once again!*

* * *

I can't do this, I thought. I'd given up hope that Mark and Mindy would make it to Don't Tell Mama's and my debut would be ruined. I tried to steel myself, say that things would be all right, that I'd make it, yes I would, and I took a deep breath. The MC signaled to me that I was next. *No way can I do this!*

Driving into work that week, I'd been practicing my act aloud in my car: *Okay Joke 1, ballplayers on strike, Joke 2 single lane only, Joke 3 E.T.* …and I thought: What if I should panic and go blank? Sure, I knew my jokes backwards and forwards, sure I had the order down pat, but could it hurt to have a contingency plan in place? So I came up with a "fail-safe" plan in case of a mental power failure. I was ready, I was confident, each of the four classes adding incrementally to that feeling of being comfortable and feeling natural in front of people.

But who would know what would happen when it came time for the real deal? No matter how I sliced and diced it, those were *practice* sessions. Firefighters run up and down props of burning buildings, but that doesn't ready them for the real thing. They get a feel for the reality of the situation, sure…but still, until you're thrust in the heat of the moment…you never really know what it's really going to be like.

My brother Berny used to tell me that the situations he went through at the New York Police Academy could never compare to what he had to face on the streets in the 1970's and 1980's.

"When I was in the academy, they used to hit us with all these situations that were nothing like the shit we'd face out there. It wasn't a movie where someone would come from out of the sky to pluck you from danger. This was the real deal, and it wasn't pretty. Through it all, though," Berny said, "I was confident I could handle most of the normal stuff."

And I was confident with my opening salvo towards fame and fortune (or, a few laughs at least) but I still wanted to enter the fray with legitimate backup in case of a blackout.

Just as I felt my life preserver slipping away and the S.S. Lazarus on the verge of sinking into the night, a sexy blond with bouffant hair swept through the double-doors like one of those girls entering a spaghetti western bar. She was wearing a bright white halter top contrasted by a black choker. All heads swept in unison towards her; and all that seemed to be missing were the fishnets, a mink stole that she could slink back over her shoulder, and the soundtrack from the movie *The Good, The Bad, and The Ugly.*

Mindy, my teleprompter had arrived! Instantly my heart rate decelerated, and I let go of the curtain.

Mark and Mindy to the rescue.

Mindy, a life-long friend and another non-believer of my plan to delve into comedy ("You know you'll never do it! You've been saying you'd do comedy for years…but you never do!"), would be stationed up front with a set of index cards that had "key words" on them. These were words that would remind me of what joke to tell and in what order. After every joke she would simply flip a card and—*voila!*—instant backup. I thought it was a good idea, similar to what my mom used to do with flip cards to help me study for vocabulary tests way back when.

When I told Mindy of her role, she was skeptical. "You didn't do too well in school, you know," she said.

What was she, a comedian?

"...And now, making his comedy debut...let's have a hand for *Steeeeeeeve Laayzarus.*"

I grabbed the mic stand away from the MC like a peeved kid taking his ball back after being left out of a pickup game, and almost took his hand with it. Thanks, Sherlock, for screwing up my last name! From there I was on automatic pilot.

Thank you thank you and good evening.

I instantly started pacing the stage like a caged tiger.

You know, I work part-time as a vendor at Yankee Stadium and I think things are gonna be a liiittle *bit different this year with the baseball strike...*

The imaginary fan pointed to me.

Hey! Two hotdogs over here!

Yeah, excuse me buddy? Watch my hotdog bin, I'll be right back, I'm up next!

Rimshot! Laughter. Oh. My. God!

Mindy demurely flipped to the next card.

E.T. it read.

How many of you guys have ever seen a porno movie?

Laughs. That was good. I can do this.

Do you know how they get the names for them? Shaking heads; bewildered looks; flushed faces, a little squirming. *I'll tell ya. What they do is, they take a regular box office hit and they give it a sorta dirty twist, ya know?* They were listening...

I think they finally hit a new low; the other day, I was walking on forty-eighth and eighth avenue and I looked up...and there it was, on the marquee: Triple X: E.T. the extra testicle.

Howls of laughter.

I was officially on my way. I'd caught the comedy bug and couldn't shake it. How was I to know what lay ahead?

* * *

I started scouring the metro area for any chance to do comedy: open mics at bars and coffee houses, Kiwanis or VFW clubs, even talent shows on, say, Jewish Singles Weekends or at local pool clubs in the summer. I wanted to perform at regular comedy clubs but no club owner wanted to feature a virtually unproven performer without a track record. Heaven forbid the paying customer didn't laugh!

Hey! Who's this Steve Laayzarus? Man does he suck!

It seemed that unless it was an open mic night at a club, most owners were hesitant to put you on stage. After all, the people at the show knew in advance that you probably sucked!

It was a real Catch-22. The club owners wanted an experienced comedian but I had none. So how was I to get experience if no one was letting me on stage? One positive was that even though I wasn't getting on stage, club owners would see my face week-after-week and every once in a while they'd let me do a few minutes. Soon, months had passed without me getting any significant stage time and, like anything else, if you don't work at a particular skill, you get rusty. I was beginning to feel like the Tin Man.

Then I had another one of those potentially fatal brainstorms: If I couldn't get stage time because no one wanted to put me on, and stage time is what I needed to get experience, how about I get stage time by putting on my own comedy show?

That was the idea. I wouldn't even charge owners to put the show on as I reasoned my "pay" was getting to work out my act in front of a live audience. Struggling comics can't put a price on working on their live act when they're starting out or, for that matter, when you're an established star.

Now all I had to do was find a business owner that was a willing guinea pig.

Enter Cobblestones, a bar among a string of watering holes in Bayside, Queens, a long stone's throw from my house. I'd frequented Cobblestones for years and I knew that in the summer they had a neat open air room in the back where patrons often migrated for a quieter meeting with friends, associates, or a floozy with a plunging neckline. It seemed like the ideal spot to perform. Just rearrange a few tables, clean up some of the vomit, and add a small stage in front of the huge seaside mural.

It took some convincing but I assured the owner that it was a win-win situation for him as we could try it once and if it didn't work, we'd both move on. Honestly, what could he lose? Especially when I told him that at least twenty of my friends and family would be around for the first show.

COBBLESTONES' COMEDY CALVACADE!
Eat, drink and laugh your damn hearts out!

Would my venture, like a boat taking on too much water, eventually sink? Would my plan for getting stage time fail?

In all probability, had I not had the good fortune of meeting fellow comedian Rich Walker in 1995 when Governor's Comedy Club on Long Island hosted Open Mike Night on Tuesdays, there's a great chance my comedy career would've been shipwrecked.

Rich, an escapee from a Buddy Hackett chain gang, his Hindenburg head ready to explode with laughter from his *own* jokes, is that 'Good Guy' that every one of us seems to have heard of though few have met. After one of the shows, which was hosted by long-time stand-up comic Peter Bales, I told Rich about my plans to start my own show and, to my surprise, he seemed genuinely happy for me.

I'd often miss working Yankee games where I could make $200–$300 in order to perform at Peter's shows, but the bastard never put me up. (How did we ever go into business together years later?) Missing games and *still* not getting stage time hurt, sure, but I later realized that it was part of "paying your dues." The fact that people saw me making the effort to try to get on a show was sometimes worth it. Plus, I did get to speak to more comics. Rich was more than helpful: be it talking with me and helping rework my jokes or encouraging me to stick it out, it gave me solace for missing Yankee games. We'd often go out to eat after shows and spend hours discussing the business or working on jokes or talking about what worked or didn't work with other comedians we might've seen on any particular night. As Yogi Berra said, "You can observe a lot by watching."

And I did.

When Rich heard my Cobblestone's brainstorm, he did something that few people would do in *any* competing business. Whereas most guys would've said of the venture, "Yeah, that's nice, buddy. Good Luck!" Rich opened up his little black book and gave me a bunch of names of comedians that might be willing to perform—for free, I hoped. Names like Murphy and Klein and Carlin and Dice Clay and....

Think about it: How many times have you heard of a virtual stranger doing that?

And in *spite* of Rich, everything pretty much worked out as I'd hoped. The Cobblestone's show ran through the Summer of '95 and I got my much needed stage time. As the host, I had the good fortune to learn from some of the people that performed there and continue to make their way in the comedy world today: Rich, Peter, Debbie Shea, Lewis Schaffer (who's since moved to England), Josh Spear, and a slew of others.

In my 10-week run as host, I learned what did and didn't work in comedy. I watched other comedians and took cues from them, both good and bad. I watched their mannerisms, their pacing, and their banter with the audience. I was cognizant of the fluctuation of their voice and subtle nuances with their hands or facial expressions or just how they reacted to audiences. I also learned how to improvise when things were out of your control: a waitress walking directly in your path or a patron walking and talking to you ("You know which way is the John?" "Yeah, across the street at Dunkin' Donuts!"). You had to be ready for anything: a spotlight that didn't work ("Comedy in the Dark; let's do it!"), a microphone that squelched without warning, a befuddled big-boobed bimbo in the front row being clueless after a punchline. These were the big little things I learned rather quickly, and it was all because of the position I was in as a host.

Instinctively, I developed an appreciation for comedians who had made it big. They *all* paid their dues just like I did. (Early on I ended up working with both Ray Romano and Kevin James before Hollywood beckoned them.) This wasn't baseball where the talent to hit a juiced up little ball far over a Little League fence had people instantly noticing you and coddling you before you could even construct a proper grammatical sentence. Good comedians are a dime a dozen and great ones can be found in just about any comedy club in America. But to make a living at it, a real living, that's a whole 'nother enchilada, and one needs to develop skin thicker than Iron Man's armor.

I learned how to pace the stage. How to hold the microphone. How not to step on my own joke. I learned how to deal with hecklers and drunks. And how to talk to your audience. I learned how to handle bombing on stage and how to deal with faulty equipment (and a few people with short circuits). The last night of the Cobblestone's show, the main speaker blew a fuse. A number of people complained they couldn't hear.

"I can't talk any louder," one comedian said. "You'll just have to listen more carefully!"

I started to understand the importance of how good common sense in business goes a long way. I thanked the comedians for their time, told them I was quite appreciative of their efforts, and hoped to see them again. Small things, like little kisses or a single rose to your main squeeze, sometimes reap large dividends.

Just speaking with so many comedians that summer gave me different takes on what did and didn't work for them and what they thought about my act. (I didn't always agree with them, but I took it all in.) I learned how changing one or two words or eliminating certain parts of a bit can changes things immensely. Someone suggested I start videotaping my performances and I'd eventually spend hours analyzing them like a batter searching for flaws in his swing. I still watch tapes today to see what works and what needs work. Looking back, it's painful to watch those early tapes.

"Ever watch those late night infomercials? Well, here's one for music from the 60's and 70's in Israel."

(Sung to the tune of The Monkees' theme)
> *Hey hey we're Hasidim*
> *People say we're schlepping around*
> *But we're too busy praying*
> *To put anybody down*

(Sung to the tune of "Rain Drops Keep Falling on My Head")
> *My yarmulke keeps falling off my head*
> *And just like the guy whose nose is too big for his head.*
> *Nothing seems to fit ...*

Sorry Mr. Sinatra, but...
> *Start spreading the lox*
> *We're noshing today...*

Just be glad that the Hasidic comic won't be in any movie or direct-to-video release. And be very happy you didn't see the top hat and long, curly sideburns in person.

Gradually, after the Cobblestone's run was over, I consistently appeared at more open mics or clubs with paying gigs. I began to see comedians that had worked at Cobblstone's and established a sort of "in" when it came time to seek more work. Fellow comics often offered a kind word to a willing club owner: "Sure, I've worked with Steve before. Funny guy...though he needs to get laid!" Word gets around fast in this business and a good word could open previously unlocked doors. Except with women.

"Yeah, Shirl, as soon as I found out he didn't have his own sitcom and he's not the general manager of the Yankees but the beer vendor, I went back to the lawyer I told ya about from Scarsdale."

* * *

In 1998, following another star-studded comedy show starring Rich, Peter and yours truly, we went out for our customary late-night snack at the Triple Crown Diner on Long Island. We got to talking about all the lousy open mic nights and how so many new comics didn't have a clue about the business or didn't know the first thing about turning their raw material into polished gems. Though we were still struggling ourselves to make headway, we all felt that we could help those that had a dream, just like us.

That's when we came up with the idea for "Stand-Up University," a college for aspiring comedians. At the end of seven weeks, those brave souls, the majority of whose jokes had been confined to office parties, family reunions and behind closed doors, would not only earn a graduation diploma for successful completion of the course, but they'd get to perform in a real New York comedy club, and have the chance to fulfill a dream (or a dare). The difference between this class and the one that I took in Manhattan was as obvious as success and failure. Plus, you got more than a broomstick and an egg timer to perform.

Peter is a college professor and a former New York radio talk show host who's been in the business for three decades. He's an alumnus of Chicago's famous "Second City" that gave us the Blues Brothers, John Belushi and Dan Akroyd, Mike Myers, Shelley Long, and Bill Murray. Rich and I are college dropouts so it seemed like a perfect fit to teach the class.

Rich is always full of great advice with our students. "*Great joke!*"

he'll say. "Now, after you say it next time, lay a big fart! That will *really* make those in the front row react!"

All of us thought it would be good to give something back. The comedy business can sometimes be downright depressing, and it's not the ideal choice for manic depressives with its rollercoaster of highs and lows. The "highs" are sometimes spectacular, and we wanted those that always dreamed of being comedians to experience a taste of that. Plus, while we worked with others on their jokes, we were also learning more and more about creating good jokes or shortening punch lines or knowing when to add a "tag" (a reference to an earlier joke). And maybe, we could even learn from the students, as well.

BE A COMEDIAN!
... and that's no Joke!

Learn the Art of Stand-Up Comedy

as acclaimed by the N.Y.Times!
Stand-Up University

INSTRUCTED BY
PROFESSIONAL COMEDIANS:
DR. PETER BALES,
RICH WALKER
& STEVE LAZARUS

TIME TO FOLLOW YOUR DREAM!

Stand-Up University is a first rate school instructed by
Professional Comedians who teach the fine art of Stand-Up Comedy.
Over this seven week course students are encouraged
to create and perform an original 5-8 minute routine
which depicts the comical essence of whom they really are.
Each week students get up on stage to work on their "act"
with exercises designed to hone their comedic skills.
On the 8th week, students will perform in TWO shows at two
of Long Island's top comedy clubs. The final week
will be a critical review of your performance as well as
graduation exercises. A videotape of your performance
will be given to you so that your first time on stage
can be remembered and treasured forever!

Up-and-coming stars like Chris Monty, Eric Tartaglione and Johnny Huff, who have performed coast-to-coast from Atlantic City to Las Vegas, got their start at Stand-Up U, as have many of the 500 students who've come through our funhouse.

* * *

As each day passes, the comedy bug gets stronger and stronger. It is my obsession: it's my addiction, my mistress, the air that allows me to breathe. *I need it.*

Each and every day I work on my routine or develop ideas for jokes. Working the Yankee games gives me a chance to work on some of my act with "willing" fans who often ask ridiculous questions.

"Do you work here?"
"Was it the uniform, the price badges, or the photo I.D. that made you think that?"

"Excuse me, can you tell me how to get to the upper deck?"
"Sure. Just go out to second base and a helicopter comes by."

When I first started doing comedy, I'd buy the day's newspaper and read it from front to back. I'd listen to the radio and scour the dial for inspirational prompts. I'd even rev up my old Zenith hi-fi and listen to old Bill Cosby records. I'd watch television and keep an ear open for things that might be a hot topic—or an absurd one—in the news and think about how I can put a funny slant on it. I'd watch a stack of videocassettes of comedians, read books by famous performers like Cosby, George Carlin, Jay Leno and Richard Pryor, and the countless books on how to be a stand-up comic or make it in show business. I'd spend hours at a time in Barnes & Noble and read the comedy books or autobiographies and write down notes. I'd take a little of this and a little of that and save it my mind's filing cabinet. (I still do this on occasion.)

Most of the books I read about comedians when I first started and those recently published (Bob Newhart, Robert Klein, Steve Martin), detailed a comic's continuous struggle, even after they were well-known, to establish a foothold in the quicksand that is comedy and how they managed to stay afloat. In a way, they were eye-opening revelations that showed me just what lay behind-the-scenes before I got there and what might be in store in the future if I keep plugging away. More than anything, though, they were inspirational because I knew others had suffered the same pitfalls, pratfalls, and pendulum swings that all stand-up comics are subject to.

As the years have steamrolled by, I've changed how I do things because it's easy to stagnate from doing the same ol' things and it's easy to get discouraged from the constant rejections. It's easy to pack it all in because sometimes it's damn hard to motivate yourself following a lousy set. But I still make it my business to do now what I did then: sit down and write for a couple of hours at a time on a yellow legal pad, chicken scratches of ideas streaming down the pages like candle wax. I still don't have a schedule with a set time where I do something each and every day—*call Mindy at 3:00 P.M. to see if she gets this joke*—but I do have an agenda on what I want to accomplish each day: learn at least one new thing, one thing that might help me to advance, one thing that might make it easier, one thing that might even be funny in my next show!

Often, upon hitting on a joke that was pure genius, I'd badger friends with the new bits—*Whaddaya mean you don't get it?*—and I just couldn't understand it when they didn't laugh as I knew it was funny…or at least thought it was.

I've often been asked why I do comedy. Before I did comedy, I imagined what it would be like to make people laugh, people I didn't even know. Once I actually experienced the sensation of what it was like to get laughs from strangers, feeling the love of an audience, their expecting you to entertain and take them away from the real world—for a few moments, anyway—it was an incredible high. There were also those sets where I was awful and wanted to quit. But in this business you get back on the horse and keep riding because as soon as you have another good set, those bad sets are quickly forgotten.

Comedy is my drug of choice. I always thought I was kind of funny. No not *ha ha* funny like Robin Williams, but quick-witted and clever. I knew I could never make it in a 9-to-5 world and I knew, eventually, that I had to make a choice.

Comedian Joey Kola once asked me: "Do you wanna be an accountant or do you wanna be a comedian?" In 2001, when I flung a cup of hot chocolate at my boss at Schultheis & Panettieri, my decision was made for me.

Anyway, I was getting tired of making calls from Yankee Stadium during day games when I was supposed to be at a client's office.

* * *

Comedy club owners are notorious for giving new comedians—and many in the business for years, too—hard times and short shrift. I experienced that and so do all comedians. We all have dreams about how we'll get them back when we become hot properties and they want us to perform at their clubs. When that lucky comedian does hit it big, real big, and becomes an "overnight sensation" (always after years and years of endless toil), club owners will step over each other to have them at their club because they envision $$$ signs and the resultant publicity. Comedians, however, no matter how old they get, are like elephants that never forget the good and the bad people they met in their struggle to survive.

And so it was with Jerry Seinfeld. Like most comedians, Seinfeld cast a skeptical eye towards club owners. They're notorious for being rude, arrogant and chintzy. *You want twenty bucks or not? And you pay for your own drinks at the bar!* Since so many younger comics are just trying to get stage time, they get away with it. But almost every comic has a story to tell about a club owner that has done him or her wrong and how they vowed to one day get back at them when they were on top of the comic heap. The problem is that only one in a million will make it to the Promised Land. The other problem is that there are only so many jobs for so many comedians and there's a lot of rejection involved, which is often tough to get used to. That's why so many aspiring comedians quit before they really ever get started.

Jerry Seinfeld, like any performer, suffered rejection when he first caught the comedy bug. When he made an appearance on *The Tonight Show Starring Johnny Carson* in 1981, his world turned upside down and he became a hot property.

The story goes that in 1999, Seinfeld, a year after completing his long-running sitcom, was coming back to Governors, a comedy club on Long Island where he had worked when he first started out. The club was only a short ride away from his childhood home in Massapequa, New York.

Certainly, Seinfeld was not immune in his early career to the *You want twenty bucks or not?* syndrome that club owners infect comics with. "I got nothing for you this week," they'll say. "Gimme a call next week." *Click!* You send out tapes and press kits to them and still, all too often, the phone doesn't ring or AOL doesn't got mail for you.

Seinfeld, though he sees things on a different level than most of us, experienced the same trials as many young comics. And like most performers, superstars or first-time stand-ups, before a show he likes to freshen up a bit, dab his face and hands with some water, do his duties, and get ready. What better place than the john? So Seinfeld had a simple request for the club owner before he'd agree to do the show: build him a bathroom. Sink, potty, mirror, the works. And make sure the hand towels are fluffy and new.

"But Jer …" said the club owner.

"My own bathroom," said Jerry. "Or you can fughedaboutit!"

Mr. Seinfeld also wanted three new top-of-the-line Shure microphones.

"But Jer…" said the club owner.

"My own bathroom," reiterated Jerry, "and the mics. Or I won't do the show. I'm not kidding."

Seinfeld got his microphones—and the bathroom, too.

In the end, he used only one of the pricey microphones and never stepped foot in the bathroom. Seinfeld did that to show all the other comics he was paying back the scummy club owner.

Who said rich guys forget where they came from?

> Why is it illegal to park in a handicapped parking space but okay to go the bathroom in a handicapped stall?
> - JERRY SEINFELD

FIFTH INNING

All in the Family

*Once you're into this family,
there's no getting out.*

-TONY SOPRANO,
The Sopranos

ON DECEMBER 24, 2007, *Newsday*, the Long Island-based daily, ran a small article in the local news section about a man, 49, that jumped in front of an express train to Jamaica, Queens, and was killed. Details were sketchy and there was never a follow-up article. It was a story that many people probably read and gave a quick thought about how holiday time is not the same for everyone.

The man who took his life was Brian Leites, a vendor who had worked at Yankee Stadium for as long as I had. (He was actually one number ahead of me in seniority.) A part of the Yankee family, his death wasn't mentioned in any team yearbook, program, or even in an end-of-year company blurb. During Old-Timers' Day, the Yankees neglected to mention Brian Leites as one of the dearly departed during their moment of reflection. Manny Gluck, a former New York City school principal and the #1 vendor before his death in 2005, and Jamie Herskowitz, Centerplate's General Manager for food services who died in 2007, both received that honor.

But not Brian.

A *Newsday* forum blogger would later write: THE TERRIBLE FRAME OF MIND HE MUST HAVE BEEN IN BREAKS MY HEART AND I HOPE HE ENJOYS A WONDERFUL AFTERLIFE. PEACE TO HIM.

The website, steveandthetank.com, would devote some kind words to Brian who worked every sports venue in New York since he was a teenager growing up in the Bronx. THE NEW YORK SPORTS WORLD LOST BRIAN LEITES OVER THE HOLIDAYS. HE WAS NEVER ON THE BACK PAGE, HE WAS NEVER MAKING HEADLINES, BUT HE DID PARTICIPATE IN EVERY PROFESSIONAL SPORTING EVENT IN THE TRI-STATE AREA OVER THE LAST 30 YEARS. HE WITNESSED SEVERAL WORLD SERIES (EVEN ONE WON BY THE METS!) AND OTHER GREAT MOMENTS. MOST LIKELY IF YOU HAVE BEEN TO A METS, YANKEES, JETS, GIANTS, DEVILS, KNICKS, NETS, RANGERS OR ISLANDERS GAME YOU KNOW HIM. HE MOST LIKELY SOLD YOU A HOT DOG OR A BEER...SO OVER THE WEEKEND, RAISE A GLASS IN HIS MEMORY. I'M SURE HE SOLD YOU SEVERAL TIMES OVER THE YEARS.

If you were ever served by Brian or ever heard his familiar voice selling his "iiiice cream! Hey, get your cold iiiiiice cream heeere!" or his Hebrew National all beef "haaat dawg! hey, haaaaat dawg here!" in his whiny, playful voice you got the feeling he was a bit different, a little out there.

* * *

As an avid Yankees fan since the 1960s, I distinctly recall one thing probably overlooked by the multitude of fans watching baseball games on the tube or listening to them on tabletop or portable transistor radios: the sounds of the game *other* than the sounds of the game. I was acutely aware of the calls of the vendors hawking their wares: soda, hot dogs, peanuts, cotton candy, Cracker Jacks, pretzels, and beer. Deep down, you sensed their desperation to unload their individual products, desperate for buyers to make an instant purchase. *Oh please buy this soda! Oh please buy this hot dog! Pleasepleaseplease my mother's in need of a major operation and if I can't get the money by the ninth inning tonight...*

Like any workplace, Yankee Stadium has its share of offbeat characters, and Brian Leites certainly fit the bill. He had a distinguishing John

Lennon tattoo on his beefy left arm, thick Coke bottle glasses, a goofy smile and always said hello to you with an even goofier trademark greeting: he'd put out his hand waiting for you to slap him "five" then pull it away just as you went for it and yell "Cheerio!" while making a circle with his thumb and forefinger and putting it in front of his eye in an "a-ok" salute. After a while, all the vendors, upon seeing Brian, would say "Cheerio!" and play along.

Some of the vendors, when they saw him, would go through the whole Cheerio! routine then follow it up by pinching his chest. *"Ooooh!"* Brian would say, thrusting his arms about him in mock protection. "You made my nipples hard! *Stop it!*"

But in quieter times, if you spoke to Brian and listened to him and to his rationale on things, listened to his take on the world and his philosophy on life, you *knew* he was smart. Plain and simple, he was a character, one of many at the House that Ruth Built.

Brian was a big part of the Animal House atmosphere that often prevails when you put 100–200 men together, often times in cramped—*very cramped*—quarters.

"Cheerio!" Brian.

* * *

The late Nick Gerardi worked into his eighties with his catchy, broken record "Get yur beer, hey beer! Get yur beer, hey beer! Get yur beer, hey beer!" His was one of those familiar sounds I heard way back when: be it under the covers in my bed, listening furtively in the earphone of my little Panasonic AM radio in Science Lab, or in between ogling the babes at Jones Beach. When I got a chance to work with Nick, it was like working with a legend. After all, here was someone I listened to for years as background music to the strains of Phil Rizzuto's "Holy Cow!" and thinking how cool it was to do that. Just how many times had I heard Nick on radio or on WPIX 11?

When I finally got to meet him during my first week at the Stadium, he was a hunched over man who came off as quiet and dignified, one of those never-bother-a-soul types. A lunch-pail guy that just picked up his beer at the commissary and…. "Get yur beer, hey beer! Get yur beer, hey beer! Get yur beer, hey beer!" I imagine he must have really loved his job to keep at it for over a half-century.

In *Hey Hotdog!* the sitcom based on this book, comedian Jerry Stiller, who played Frank Costanza on *Seinfeld* and has been in show business since 1956, has already signed on the dotted line to play Nick Gerardi. The Brooklyn-born Stiller is a perfect fit for Nick's vendor role having played "loudmouth" Arthur Spooner in *The King of Queens.* He was recently spotted in the WPIX archives digging up those long-ago tapes and has reportedly been practicing his beer call at his New York home. "I've already sold a few six-packs to my neighbors," said Stiller.

A vendor at a ballpark is, for all intents and purposes, a salesman. He's got an item to sell and one that most people want, regardless of the outrageous price. Fans have to eat and drink, no?

Eight-fifty for a beer?
I can get a whole six-pack for that!
Not here you can't! But for a buck, I'll give you a sip.

The way a vendor "pushes" his product can often make or break a sale. Many people have been known to buy from a certain vendor because of the "fun factor"—like throwing a bag of peanuts a la Jaba Chamberlain or because, on a hot and steamy New York kind of day, one vendor will use his portable fan to spritz water on the customer as well. Another vendor makes sure that whenever he sees someone taking a picture, he always makes sure he becomes a part of it. He's never offended anyone and the people want him in the snapshot. (It must be the uniform.) Think of advertisers adding a little glitter to their everyday products with fancy packaging or promotions.

Soap on a rope! What a clean way to have fun!

At the Stadium, many vendors take the Brian Leites approach, adding an elongated vowel or dramatically stressing a consonant or hawking their product rapid-fire. *Hey, get your soda soda soda!!*

And others have even stranger ways of selling their stuff.

Take Norman Jaffe. Norman's approach is, shall we say, a bit offbeat. Some might even think he's "lost it." Jaffe's been at the Stadium since the 1980's. Many people think that Norman is really "Jerome," a constant, passionate and thoroughly irritating caller to the WFAN All-Sports Radio Station in New York that fans love to hate. Within seconds of calling the station, Norm, uh Jerome, will start yelling into the telephone.

"The Yankees gotta get rid of that bum! Every time he comes into the game, he blows the lead! It's de-spic-able and I'm tired of him! I TELL YA I CAN'T TAKE IT ANYMORE!"

Steve Sommers, one of the hosts on WFAN, precedes Norm, uh Jerome's call, by playing the *Twilight Zone* theme.

. . . Doo Doo Doo Doo, Doo Doo Doo Doo . . .

Funny, but Norman will act the same way if you're having a "normal" conversation with him and he simply disagrees with what you're saying. He'll start waving his hands all over the place like a crack-fueled traffic cop and rail, "Oh you're such an idiot! What do you know? Why do I even waste my time talking to you? You're such a dick!" Sometimes he'll go off on a tirade, spittle flying in all directions, and sometimes he'll just go off into the sunset (or in the direction of the bleachers). Either way, you gotta love him as he's as harmless as bellybutton lint.

While many vendors simply turn the product they're selling into their own mellifluous melody, Norman, in his powerfully gruff and frog-like voice, will have none of that. Shirt untucked, baggy pants dragging along the ground, crumpled vendor's hat askew and, on a summer's day sweat pouring down his face like someone left the water running, Norman will hawk his product pronouncing it *backwards.*

"Daz Haagen here! Get yur Daz Haagen here! Jack Crack here!"

And the fans love it. They laugh at his backwards antics and how he scurries all discombobulated up and down an aisle like a mouse caught in a maze. The fans will smile at each other when a fellow vendor eyes Norm's uniform shirt plastered to his back from that day's heat and humidity and razzes him. "Hey Norman, get caught in a shower? You need a towel?"

Granted, the fans can't be too crazy about getting Norm's sweat on them, but at least he doesn't sell hot dogs on those days where the vendor's sweat gets mixed in with the steaming hot dog juice.

Ugh.

You'd think that all the vendors come from the tri-state New York area, and most do. But not all.

Direct from the City of Brotherly Love it's Howard Tannebaum, better known as "The Rabbi." Each and every game he travels from his home in Philadelphia via the Penn Central Railroad. It's a wonder that between how little product he sells and the cost of a round-trip train ticket for each game, he even eats. To look at The Rabbi, your first impression is that of a homeless vagabond, one who sets up shop under the FDR Drive.

Like the Liberty Bell, the Rabbi is a bit cracked.

He'll talk to people when they're not listening, mumble something that makes no sense, and then answer his own questions after someone just mumbles back, "Yeah, I know." Without prompting he'll spout selected biblical passages to those within earshot as if those in attendance might have a Hebrew proficiency exam in the morning.

If The Rabbi heard that someone was caught sneaking in a few extra hot dog buns, bags of peanuts or Twizzlers to sell, or if a banker was found to be dipping into his till, he might spout:

Then Joshua and all Israel with him, took Achan the son of Zerah, the silver, the mantle, the bar of gold, his sons, his daughters, his oxen, his donkeys, his sheep, his tent and all that belonged to him; and they brought them up to the valley of Achor. And Joshua said, "Why have you troubled us? The LORD will trouble you this day." And all Israel stoned them with stones; and they burned them with fire after they had stoned them with stones.

The Rabbi can usually be found before the game scrambling about the vendor's locker room trying to get his act together. He'll frantically search his dime-store bags for his keys or the roll of quarters that he needs for change or sit frustrated in front of his locker because he's forgotten the combination. Then he'll ask, "Steve, did you see my ID badge?"

During the game—and you can't make this up—The Rabbi will crouch in the aisle using his little TEXAS INSTRUMENTS calculator and figure out what a fan owes him for his purchase.

"Let's see, you bought two Lemon ices for your kids, one for your wife and…"

In a show of thanks following each sale, he'll tip his sweat-stained cap and reveal a multi-colored, ornately embroidered New York Yankees yarmulke with the interlocking NY smack-dab in the center of it. The skull cap barely covers stringy wisps of salt-and-pepper hair and severely pockmarked skin.

Of course, The Rabbi can only work until sundown on Fridays, but he's currently petitioning the Yankees to make all Friday games afternoon games.

You know what game I want to see?
Jewish Monopoly.
Can you imagine the chance cards?
Advance to Boardwalk, accidental slip and fall
in hotel lobby, collect 2.3 million.

Then there's Baltimore, the vendor not the city. The vendors nicknamed Roderick Coleman "Baltimore" because that's where he lives. His nickname, though apropos location-wise, doesn't quite fit his persona. Like The Rabbi, Baltimore makes the trek here for each game when he's not working at Camden Yards, home of the Baltimore Orioles. In both parks, it seems that Baltimore spends more time soliloquizing than selling.

Rumor has it that one of the red bricks used to build the O's home field came loose in the Camden Yards concourse on Opening Day and befell the beefy vendor. Or maybe, as one Yankee vendor who requested anonymity said, "Someone probably just threw a brick at his head." It's assumed the blow to the head caused some kind of imbalance. Soon after, Baltimore started foaming at the mouth with his daily soliloquies, spoken any time or any place without prior warning, be it at Camden Yards or Yankee Stadium or 42nd and Broadway or in the middle of a crowded Metroliner, for all I know.

At the Stadium, he's famous for announcing that day's starting lineups. "Leading off for the Yankees," he'll say in a fair imitation of Bob Sheppard, public address announcer at the Stadium for the last 50 years, "Number two, Derek Jeter." He'll even throw in the reverb from the loudspeaker so it will come out "Number two, Derek Jeter...Jeter... Jeter..." Baltimore will take you through the entire lineup before the game, as fans listen, first in disbelief and then in rapt attention, and trade puzzling glances (and a skeptical smile) at his wackiness.

During any given game he'll stop wherever he happens to be: in front of dichards in the box seats as a Yankee steps up to the plate needing a homerun to tie the score, in front of a fan on a stairway trying to balance cups of foaming beers on a thin cardboard tray, or alongside a line for the bathroom. He'll set down his bin of Cracker Jacks or pretzels or peanuts, stand ramrod straight, and announce, "Ladies and Gentleman, now batting, number fif-ty fiiive, Hideki Matsui...Matsui...Matsui..."

I'm sure some fans experience a bit of panic or paranoia as Baltimore's Barney Google eyes sometimes bore right into them and it seems that nothing short of Stadium security blindfolding, gagging and cuffing him and depositing him in Creedmore—can stop him from booming out the entire lineup.

And then he just might go into a rant on something far-removed from the baseball diamond.

"The president has gotta do something about this gas crisis! It's making all the prices go up up UP! How can a family of four afford to drive to Yankee Stadium in their SUV if it costs them a hundred bucks just to fill up? And who gets hurt? ME! They can't buy from me because they left all their money at the pump! And what if they have a Hummer? That monstrous thing gets seven miles to the gallon! And how many soldiers are dying unnecessarily, the victims of roadside bombs? I say General Motors needs to recall all the Hummers of the world with the soldiers still in 'em! Let those poor soldiers come right here and I'll give 'em free beer for their troubles! Hummer owners won't like this but we'll give them bicycles in return for their exhaust-belching, environment-polluting stink bombs! THOSE ARE THE REAL KILLERS! HAS ANYONE CHECKED THE OZONE LAYER LATELY??"

Then, if it was, say, the start of the sixth inning he'd go silent as the Stadium groundskeepers got ready to lead the crowd into a frenzy with their rendition of the Village People's "YMCA" dance.

Even if Baltimore is selling a beer, in between measured pours, he'll start viciously bopping his head in tune with the music and, on key, start singing in his gruff and scratchy voice, his beady eyes scanning the crowd for the next beer sale like a spectator at a ping pong tournament.

Young man, there's a place you can go.
I said, young man, when you're short on your dough.
You can stay there, and I'm sure you will find
Many ways to have a good time.

BOP BOP BOP BOP BOP

It's fun to stay at the Y-M-C-A.
It's fun to stay at the Y-M-C-A.

Then Baltimore would do a one-handed version of "YMCA" while doling out the brews.

They have everything for you men to enjoy,
You can hang out with all the boys...

Weird shit.

Ray Bradbury has his version of the "Illustrated Man" and so do the Yankee vendors.

Jay Gottfried, a squat bull of a man with a bumpy and badly shaved head, a Goose Gossage goatee, Popeye arms, and a tattooed body that would amaze even Bradbury, has a bit smaller jaunt to work than both The Rabbi and Baltimore. He simply changes out of his starched, tight-fitting New York City court officer's uniform, slips into a pair of gym shorts and tank top (a combination that he wears despite the thermometer readings), and hops aboard his trusty Schwinn ten-speed and cycles to work, which happens to be right across the street. See that white building over there? Following the game, he uses his trusty steed to ride home to Queens.

While athletes will do calisthenics prior to a game—stretching, running, squats, push-ups and jumping jacks—Jay has his own pregame rituals: he'll secure his bike to a train trestle under the elevated line that runs next to the Stadium and do a short series of quick leg thrusts and stretch like he's an intense competitor in a game of Twister. Following that, he'll go for a leisurely run around the ballpark, say about twenty times. Nicknamed "Stinky" by his fellow vendors, Jay will then bring his stench straight into the locker room like Linus carrying his blanket. He'll change into his vending uniform, his body slick with sweat, his nipple ring twinkling in the dulled light, and grumble incoherently to himself.

And every homestand it seems like Jay shows up with a fresh patchwork of tattoos that's been added to his crazy-quilt body.

He's covered from head to toe with the highly detailed art and, it seems, so is every visible extremity. His wrists are covered, his back is a swirl of tattoos, as are the front and back of his legs. He's an Andy Warhol Pop Art in motion.

Jay's got a stark black tattoo in tribute to 9/11—"NEVER FORGET"—with a NYC fireman and policeman saluting each other over a flag-draped casket; a spread-eagled bat that drapes his powerful biceps and, because of his strategic placement (us vendors ain't all that stupid!), it looks like it's flying whenever he's moving (and shirtless). A comic book and movie fan since he was a kid, Jay's got a colorful tattoo on his right leg of the Amazing Spiderman standing over a squirming villain that's been slimed with Peter Parker's signature web goo and a pretty cool *Men in Black* tattoo featuring silhouetted characters of Will Smith and Tommy Lee Jones with huge amped-up futuristic guns at the ready. He even has Lady Justice, depicted with sword, scales, and blindfold, in tribute to his court job.

And what properly attired Illustrated Man doesn't have a "Mom" tattoo? He's got one of those too, only this one doesn't have the usual MOM lettering surrounded by a big fat red heart and colorful bouquets of flowers. Nope, this one has an actual picture of his dearly departed mother.

"I made sure not to have mom too near the naked woman," the Illustrated Man said. "I don't think she would've liked that very much."

Smart man, that Stinky.

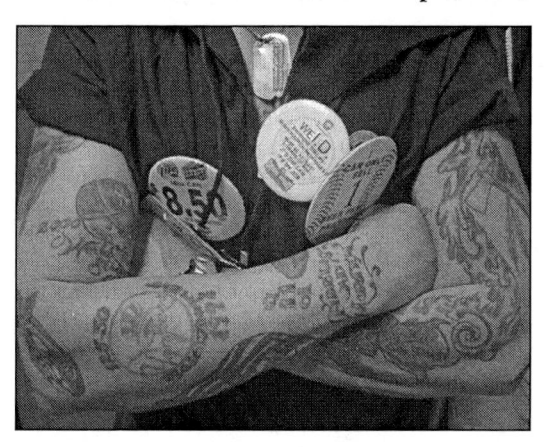

Yes, characters at the Stadium come in all shapes, sizes, and nationalities. From the 6'9" African American Riker's Island correction officer with a big stick, to the Markel Brothers, a pair of 4' Mini-Me vendors that have an affinity for selling Cracker Jacks with speech impediments that make them as hard to understand as computer code. The Markel Brothers' combination tiny heads, nasal voices, and uniforms that are at least two sizes too big, lend a comedic look to their selling.

Rick Goldfarb, who started working at Yankee Stadium in 1972 when Thurman Munson was behind the plate and the late Bobby Murcer led the team with a .292 batting average, is a senior vendor with his own shtick. For Rick, selling beer's the thing, no doubt about it, but it's not just about the decent buck he makes, which could be upwards of three-hundred per game.

Years ago Rick dubbed himself "Cousin Brewski" and his good-natured banter: "Thanks for catching a buzz from the Cuz," has helped the affable vendor establish long-lasting bonds with thousands of loyal customers (sometimes to the chagrin of fellow vendors). Many of his fans, whether they come to a ballgame once-a-week or make it to just one game a year, will specifically ask for him so they can schmooze and booze with the Cuz. At one time, Brewski even gave out personalized buttons only to see management put the kibosh on that. "I've seen 'em on eBay," he said. "The last one went for about eleven bucks."

Goldfarb will schmooze with fans all night long, losing commissions in the process, but that's not what it's all about for him. He simply loves to schmooze.

Brewski will converse on anything from politics, the current state of the Yankees, or just inquire about the goings-on of a son or daughter away in college. All done with the utmost sincerity and interest. "Hey, who doesn't like attention?" Cousin Brewski has often said.

"Best job in the world, best fans in the world, what's there not to love?" he'll tell anyone within earshot.

If you ever wanted to find Cousin Brewski, you can ask for him or just look for the vendor in the lower boxes, whistling a catchy tune or tipping his hat in thanks to a generous fan while singing a Broadway number.

Or look for the rare vendor that's in no hurry to make the next sale.

For the most part, the majority of vendors that work at ballparks and arenas use vending as supplemental income to their jobs as teachers, actors, accountants, architects, correction officers, office assistants, bartenders, messengers, truck drivers, or as a transitional job as they work their way through college. There are a select number of vendors that will work venues in a small radius, like Brian Leites did in working Yankee and Shea Stadiums, as well as Madison Square Garden, and grind out a decent living. Vendors come from all walks of life, from a slew of different countries, and with a wide spectrum of dreams for the future.

Some vendors even have aspirations for Hollywood, like the Screen Actors Guild triumvirate of Yankee Stadium: Keith Edwards, Bobby McKay, and Stuart Zully.

While they're all working towards their big Hollywood break, they're scampering up and down the cramped aisles until their next casting call. Keith, a refugee from a futuristic masquerade ball, loves to show porno on his RCA flip-phone screen as everyone is getting dressed in the locker room. *"Pssst! Yo! Yo! Yo guys! C'mere! C'mere! Check this out!"*

It's hilarious as a bunch of us gather around this tiny screen to watch grainy shadows go at it. We never knew if one of those silhouettes was actually Keith, even if he said it was.

"Yo yo yo. This is some Asian chick I met doing a rap video…oh man she was *hot!*"

Prior to working, Keith might be decked out in full black leather garb accentuating his smooth, heavily muscled brown skin, skin-tight jeans and a tight top that clings to his washboard abs like a layer of extra skin. He'll top off his eclectic fashion-statement-of-the-day assemblage with anything from aviator goggles with a few cigars stuck under its elastic bands, huge vampire teeth, Herman Munster-like eight-inch clogs, six watches on one arm, or spiked hair that looks like if you got impaled on it, only the Jaws of Life could free you. One time he showed up at work—post 9/11—in a colorful Green Beret uniform with a flak jacket visible beneath it. He looked like a real-life action figure, his camouflaged uniform consisting of helmet, oversized mirrored glasses, an empty gun belt and a bandolier swung across his chest. He was turned away from the gate and told to come back for the next game.

Supposedly Keith's made a few music videos with Queen Latifah and Lil' Kim and scored a few plum film roles too. The trouble is those films just haven't seen the light of day yet and he remains undiscovered, a microburst of energy whose vendor legend grows with each passing home game and costume change.

It's kind of funny to see the stark before and after difference when Keith puts on a simple vendor's uniform. He's barely recognizable from before, having lost all that height and all that attention. Like so many here, though, Keith retains a bit of his quirky character when he's out in the stands, even though most of it might be hidden like his ripped double-barreled chest below his flak jacket.

A flak jacket for a baseball game?

"Yo yo yo man, this is the South Bronx, son," he'll say. "I don't want no crazy fan coming out and stabbing me because his beer was warm." Rest assured, by the end of the game Keith's back to being Keith, action figure and all.

Stewart Zully and Bobby Mckay are a bit more screen accomplished than Keith and a lot more reserved. Zully's got an impressive resume with acting appearances in 35 television shows including *Hill Street Blues, Murder She Wrote, Columbo, Law and Order* and *The Sopranos*. McKay has also been on *Law and Order* and *The Sopranos* and had small parts in films like *Ladder 49*, with John Travolta, and *We Own the Night*. In that crime drama, Bobby played a guard at Riker's Island. (Some of the vendors recognized the place firsthand.)

Zully starred in a Citibank spot that won an Emmy in 2004 as "Best Commercial of the Year." He played "Jake B.", a slovenly middle-aged man plopped in a recliner who discovers that he's an identity theft victim of a, ya know, California-type bimbo. Through the magic of voice-over she's babbling on and on about the joys of spending on Jake's card, including the purchase of a $1500 leather bra that's left her overjoyed. "It lifts and separates!"

A funny thing happened to Zully on his way to Grumman's Chinese Theater: in 1994, he had a small role in the movie *Wolf,* starring Jack Nicholson. Imagine: one week this master thespian is trading barbs with a screen legend on the set of your basic multi-million dollar

Tinseltown production—only to find the next week he's offering craggy old Jack a beer at the Stadium in one of the box seats.

How amazing is that?

Centerplate is not without its Hollywood glamour girls, either. On our set we even have the female version of Louie De Palma of the hit television show *Taxi*. Our supervisor, Jean, 4'6" and 200 lbs., waddles around like a penguin on happy feet, and only appears at roll call to tell us "inspirational" news.

No one can really see her as she mounts a makeshift podium. One hundred vendors surround her. She's careful to avoid the dripping water from the overhead pipes.

"Um, uh, the Yankees are getting a lot of letters from fans," she'll say as vendors start to roll their eyes and yawn. Ho hum.

"It seems that a number of you are not giving back proper change—or any change at all. This has to stop! Also, the Yankees are telling us that vendors have been selling more than one beer per person or they're cursing in front of fans." Snickering and murmuring abound. "This has got to stop!"

"Like I said," Jean tells us, now just a drowned out dissipating voice to those that are still listening in the space big enough to house a pair of Volkswagens. "The Yankees are getting letters and they're not happy!"

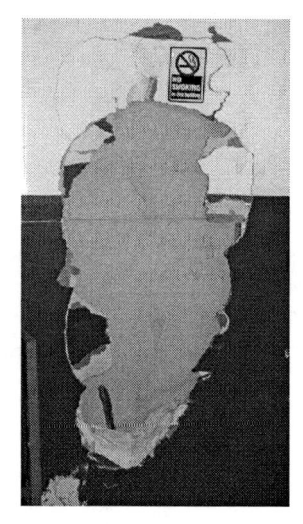

Uh, Jean, when you speak to the Yankees, can you tell them about the gaping hole in the vendor's locker room, the one with layers of vendors' clothing that have been stuffed in there and are growing fungus? Or, Jean, maybe you can let the Yankees know about the exposed asbestos pipes overhead from which showers of lead paint rain on us like parade confetti when the fans start jumping up and down in excitement? Or maybe you can inform the vaunted Yankee brass about the lone bench that was removed from the locker room two years ago, the only place where vendors can rest their weary bones after a 96° day. Can you also let them know that the steel clamps and screws that were once attached to that bench are still there, sticking out of the ground like stalagmites?

Can ya tell them that for us? Please, can ya? Don't the Yankees read any of the *vendor's* letters?

Yes, there are eight million stories in the naked city and some incredible ones right here involving the vendors and the behind-the-scenes action at the Stadium. There's a wide swath of characters with diverse interests, backgrounds and goals that are enough to fill a chapter in a book—or a weekly television show.

Did I mention Brian Samuels, who works for FedEx and has vended here for a long time despite kidney problems so severe that he has a tube permanently implanted in his arm so he can receive dialysis treatment twice a week?

Talk about guts!

Talk about *Hey Hotdog!* being a hit sitcom!

Now that's entertainment!

SIXTH INNING

A Day in the Life

Let's play two!
- ERNIE BANKS

MY VERSION OF A DAY-NIGHT doubleheader is vending in the afternoon and comedy at night. A Yankee game during the day; stand-up in the evening. Unfortunately, that's when hecklers seem to follow me around like shadows.
  Yo! I didn't pay no fifty bucks to see your ass! I wanna see A-Rod!
  Yo, Lazarus!... You ain't no Robert Klein!

Double duty doesn't happen as often as I'd like it to, but when it does, I look forward to it. It's fun. It's demanding. It's a living.

* * *

The baseball season dawns around the first week of February when vendors get an "official letter" from Centerplate telling us, in essence, if you want your vending job back, *C'mon down!* to get your new badge.

Of course, should you forget to bring in any of the following items: last year's badge, your original Social Security card, a passport that shows you're legally in the country or a driver's license that says you are who you claim to be, the Xeroxed copy of the official *C'mon down!* letter and the original store-stock envelope it came in, a ballpoint pen to sign all the official company forms, handbooks and rules and regulations, any old uniforms that you might have used as dust rags over the winter, and two bucks to pay for the processing of a new badge, you're out-of-luck: NO ADMITTANCE!

But you don't understand, you tell one of the supervisors after you've been denied admittance for the grievous sin of having everything but the original store-stock envelope that the sacred "official letter" came in. No, you don't understand, he says. Don't you see? he says pointing to the list of required items to gain admittance to get your job back. It says *right here*, spittle flying everywhere as he emphatically pokes the clipboard with the official checklist. NO ADMITTANCE! without *all* of the above.

But how will I be able to practice my new comedy routines on captive fans? How will I be able to beat them for change or curse in front of them or mix it up with the fans because they can't see A-Rod strike out with the bases loaded? Sorry, the sheriff says, but them there's the rules, son. But you've seen me every day for the last twenty years! Don't matter, the company gunslinger says. Just turn your sorry cowboy ass around and start digging through the neighborhood dumpster to find that valuable envelope! You mean the torn and gummed letter that I mistakenly threw away because I've been conditioned for my whole stupid life to rip open a United States postal letter, carefully unfold the inner part, and then throw the envelope that shielded its possible valuable contents from rain or hail or sleet or bird droppings before it reached my mitts? So now, for as long as I can remember, I'll carefully slit open the official Centerplate letter like a doctor readying a human blowfish for liposuction, and then start to gather up the plethora of items so I can embark on a new baseball season.

In the interim, I'd shake off a winter's worth of baseball cobwebs doing stretching exercises that I hadn't done since the close of last season; consider the affect that an added twenty pounds might have on my vending speed and stamina; and dig out the oversized duffel bag with my vendor's gear.

> *Is there anything that can evoke spring better than the sound of the ball smacking into the pocket of the big mitt, the sound of the bat as it hits the horsehide; for me…almost everything I know about spring is in it—the first leaf, the jonquil, the maple tree, the smell of the grass upon your hands and knees, the coming into flower of April.*
>
> - THOMAS WOLFE

April is soon upon us and, with it, the start of the season. As always, Opening Day is a festive occasion. The media—newspapers, radio, television, websites, and internet bloggers—have escalated the beginning of Baseball Season to a fever pitch. Stan's Sports Bar, just across the street from the Stadium, is hopping with activity at 9:00 a.m. Cops have set up saw horses, outside vendors have set up souvenir stands stocked with the latest and greatest Yankee paraphernalia—multi-colored Yankee hats, bobblehead dolls of the newest multi-million dollar acquisitions, dark blue jerseys with players' names on the back (unlike the traditional nameless jerseys that the players wear both home and on the road), autographed replica baseballs, pennants, giant "We're #1" foam fingers, and dozens of other items. Fans mill about like shoppers searching for a newly opened checkout line: some are already drunk, some perfectly sober but caught up in the intoxicating atmosphere, others looking to score tickets from scalpers that are already out in full force despite the sign that says: NO SCALPING TICKETS WITHIN 1500 FEET OF STADIUM. (The Stadium is a sacrifice bunt away.) The scalpers busily mark off their territory like junkyard dogs and dare others to infringe on their space. Meanwhile, vendors report over at Gate 2, go through a new round of security measures, and head into the bowels of the Stadium on their way to the locker room…and away we go!

Before you know it, the games have passed by in quick succession and …

Saturday, June 21, 2008
Yankees vs. Cincinnati Reds
VENDOR STEPS
(as outlined in the Centerplate manual)

1. Vendors report to the employee's entrance and wait until call time.

It used to be a quick 20-25 minute trip from my house in Bayside, some thirteen miles away, to the employee entrance at the Stadium, but all that ended with the Yankees' winning ways. Big crowds, constant construction on the highways and arteries leading into the South Bronx, and the construction of the new Yankee Stadium has made the drive on most days an agonizing one. By the time I navigate the constantly changing landscape, find a place to park in a different time zone and walk to the park, it's taken anywhere from 45 to 90 minutes. Call time for any game is from three hours prior to game time until 90 minutes before the start.

Today's game is a 1:05 p.m. start so vendors can report to work anywhere from 10:00 a.m. until 11:30. However, union vendors like me can come in as late as a half-hour before the start of the game providing they filled out a vendor's card the game before.

2. **Management then calls in union vendors who get a hawker card; the vendor fills out name, social security #, and seniority number and product and commissary choices on back.**

(And don't forget to include your last will and testament.)

I can still remember how long it took before I had enough seniority to sell beer. It wasn't until my 10th year, 1987, the year I joined the union, Local 153. Selling beer now is just about automatic as each and every game is sold out (over 50,000 strong) and management employs upwards of 60–70 beer vendors per game. I'm vendor # 50, so do the math. I choose to sell beer most nights in the lower level boxes ("the field") because that's easiest on the legs and you can usually do seven to 10 cases a night, making anywhere from $300 to $400 a game. Where can you make that kind of dough and test your comedy material at the same time?

3. **Depending on how many (other) vendors are needed, management proceeds to call in vendors by the year they were hired.**

It used to be that newer vendors had to sweat out that they'd get called to work during "shape-up." During the 1980s and early 1990s the Yankees drew anywhere from 12,000 to 25,000 fans for a regular season game. Management would look at the expected crowd numbers and put to work as many vendors as they felt necessary. That's what I went through when I first started. I'd stand in the crowd with other new hires—sometimes in the pouring rain and absolute freezing cold—and my insides would be crying out like Arnold Horshack of *Welcome Back Kotter* fame.

"Oooh oooh! Pick me! Pick me!"

No more. There aren't even enough vendors to work the overflow crowds and it seems they're willing to take anyone with a pulse. "We've run out of people to hire from the Bronx," Jean the Penguin once said. Newer vendors start out earning commissions of 10% while some vendors who've been here since the 1960s earn upwards of 19% a game *and* an incredible 50% bonus for the year.

4. After cards are complete, vendors hand the card back to management. The cards are then put in seniority order; union first, then by the year hired.

Then it's time to actually enter baseball's hallowed cathedral.

5. Vendors then proceed to the locker room, get dressed, and then wait in the designated call area.

Before 9/11, walking into the Stadium was as simple as showing your badge. It took a few seconds, tops. You could bring in your friendly neighborhood crack dealer and most people wouldn't bat an eyelash. Today, it's a lot different. "Yo man, don't you know you can't be bringing in no paper clip? Damn, how many times do we have to tell you vendors no sharp objects?"

Now it all depends on who's in charge of security that day.

Sometimes the entrance is patrolled by New York City Police with bomb-sniffing dogs and Stadium security. Other times a couple of people from security will use hand-held scanners if the bigger airport-style scanner is on the fritz (which is often), and give you a pat-down. They check for contraband: paper clips, letter openers, laser pens, toiletry bags. *What you got in here, man?* One time I couldn't come in with one of those eyeglass screwdrivers. The screwdriver was as big as my pinky. (Thank you, Osama.)

"I ain't in the mood for no bullshit today," growls one of the female toy cops. Her harelip twitches at the earliest sign of resistance from a worker that still hasn't grown accustomed to body searches by anyone other than their intimate partner. She's clearly taken a liking to her pre-game power trip. It's an energy drink for sure. "Have your belts *off!* Make sure your cell phones and keys and change are out of your pockets! And don't forget to swipe your badge!"

And don't even dare to try to bring in your stuff in anything but a clear bag! Oh no no no! Don't even try to bring in your briefcase from work or your soda from the bodega or an extra pair of laces for your Pro Keds. Oh no no no! They'll be confiscated at the door and you'll be paddle-whipped and given a severe tongue-lashing. "But I'm coming from work and these are Top Secret government papers! The security of the nation is at stake!"

"Sorry, just dump it in that blue bin over there, the one with all the other stuff that the idiot vendors tried to bring in."

Forget your badge? *Tsk! Tsk!* Guess who might not be working today? Like all of a sudden thirty-year veterans were going to be contacted by Osama bin Laden and his operatives and ordered to hide a plastic bomb in their utility belts. *Incredibly,* the fans are subjected to a mere touch-and-go and basically zip through the turnstiles. No X-rays no scanners, just a quick check of the pocketbooks and Enjoy the Game!

Either way, it's amazing how a group of nefarious people could change the world forever.

— — —

There are some guys that wait until the last minute to get dressed. They can do it one-two-three and they're ready to rock. (Keith Edwards isn't one of them.) There are others that need a little more time as they lay their uniform out nice and neat, methodically pack up all their clothes in squared bundles, and then squeeze their stuff into small, decrepit and rusty lockers that were probably there when Babe Ruth was munching on hot dogs in the Yankees dugout. Most of the lockers are broken. Their frames are bent so wickedly out of shape you'd think some irate vendor took a sledgehammer to 'em when he found they were out of 52XXX pants. On any given day you might find shards of a broken fluorescent light bulb brushed off into a corner, used latex gloves, empty candy wrappers or newspapers in and around the lockers, all destined to stay there for a long time. We've learned to tiptoe around the piles of dirty clothes that pile up like peas on a plate.

(As you can see from the picture of the Yankees' locker room, all locker rooms are not created equal.)

When I get dressed in our private luxury box, it's a whole routine, just like my comedy act. If I think about it, it just ain't funny. The fact is that all these years vending, the pounding—bam! bam! bam!—have taken its toll, both mentally and physically.

How many times have I tried to get size 36 pants during the first game of a homestand only to be told by the woman that speaks broken English, "Sorry, senor, n-no pant." I used to argue with her. "*How can't there be any pants? It's the* first *game!*" "We have, you know, 40's," she'll say. I'll shake my head and take them. "I don't get it," I mumble to myself. "I just don't."

Now I just keep my 36's and wash them out every night. It saves me agita.

I walk towards the locker room and pass vendors and hi-five and fist bump them. There a few New York City cops in the area as there's a small holding cell around the corner from our locker room where fans are escorted for disorderedly conduct like inciting the crowd or running on the field or scalping tickets. How dare they scalp tickets when fans can get Yankees' tickets from eBay or Stub Hub at exorbitant prices? Then I make my way around the traffic jam of police scooters and bicycles, scorecard stands, beer portables with collapsed umbrellas, and hot dog carts with scores of condiment packets stuck together from the heat and humidity.

On this homestand, a hidden pipe has sprung a leak and you tiptoe through huge puddles of muddied water with cigarette butts and mustard and ketchup packets floating about like psychedelic waterbugs. Some genius decided that this would be the perfect place to make the storage area.

Joe, over here with all that stuff! There's plenty of room! It's only the vendors' locker room!

 Entering the U-shaped locker room, you squeeze by vendors playing poker. There's guaranteed to be a small crowd there every game and the requisite cigarette and cheap Tiparillo smoke wafting towards the ceiling, the remnants of tobacco having seeped into a patchwork of vendors' clothes tied around a huge exposed pipe that has turned a ghastly shade of brown from the seepage of rusted water. Were the clothes put there to actually stop a leak—or as a gag? Its size grows exponentially each year.

I walk into one of three locker rooms where we dress; it's the size of a small self-storage facility and it's filled wall-to-wall with battleship gray lockers that have huge dents and dings indicating that players take batting practice here when we're on the road. The linoleum is cracked and some of it peels up around the lockers leaving splinters of wood climbing the walls like Wrigley Field ivy. The monstrous hole in the wall looks as enticing as ever. I start to open my combination lock and immediately have to glance at the numbers I scribbled on the wall next to me (34–22–28) because I've forgotten them. As I start to unload my gear, the characters for *Hey Hotdog!*, the future Emmy Award-winning sitcom, begin to file in.

Keith Edwards is there with his phone and he's into his *Yo yo yo!* Norman Jaffee shuffles in bitching about how the Yankees need to trade for a real centerfielder. Marlon Jackson, a 6'4" Jamaican with a huge afro and a gold chain as thick as corded rope, struts in a little late. "Ahh, mon, that fuckin new stadium construction fuckin me up, mon. I hod to walk eight fuckin blocks and I just hope my niggaz don't be fuckin with my wheels."

Usually nobody understands a word he says—I don't know how he sells anything!—but the vendors all love him because he's got the best pot.

Only in the last few years has the time it's taken me to get dressed been as long as Old Timers' Day ceremonies. When I first started in 1977 I'd put on my 32 pants and medium smock, fasten my ID badge and vendors' buttons, adjust my hatband and, in two minutes, I'd head outside to await call.

"Lazarus, peanuts in the bleachers!"

"*Damn!* Will I ever get hot dogs or beer?"

Yesterday, Vendor #2711; thirty-one years later, The Beer Man. Vendor #50.

And it only took two Popes, two All-Star games, six World Championships, and a partridge in a pear tree to get here.

Finally it's time to get dressed.

"Lazarus, move your shit!" says fat Joe Schmidt, the Iron Horse of the Yankee vendors having worked an astonishing *twelve hundred* straight games. (John Goodman will easily fit not only into Joe's pants but into his role on *Hey Hotdog!*) Having to work alongside Joe is one thing for the last twenty years, but can we talk?

Have you ever seen a man in a size 52 pants naked?

"C'mon, Laz, let's move the stuff!"

The first thing I do is put on my knee brace. Then I put Desitin where the sun don't shine to prevent rashes from the sweat. Today's game temperature will rise to 77°. Then I sprinkle on some Johnson's Baby Powder and push Fat Joe aside for some room while I put on two pairs of socks leaning against my locker because I guess the Yankees still don't know about the missing bench. Now I put on my large shirt and pants, my elbow brace, spray Biofreeze on my neck in hopes of preventing any pain later, cram a bunch of Chloraseptic throat lozenges in my pocket, and dry-swallow three Advil.

Then I do my game-day exercises: I try to touch my toes a few times, work out the kinks in my neck, do a few cartwheels around the locker room, pass the medicine ball around with the other vendors, and I'm done. All this takes around 20 minutes. Some days it takes a little longer if I have to take Claritin D if my allergies are acting up or Prilosec for my acid reflux.

On the other side of the room I hear the Markel Brothers speaking in their own language and soon after smell Jay "Stinky" Gottfried before he actually walks in the room. The Illustrated Man shows off a new tattoo, this one of a B-51 Mustang Bomber like one that his uncle flew in WWII.

"How's the book coming, Laz?" says Gottfried. "Not bad," I say.

"Don't forget, you said you'd get a shot of me and my new nipple ring!"

The Rabbi isn't here because it's Saturday and he doesn't work the Sabbath.

6. **In the meantime, management fills out the staffing sheet by what the union vendors have written on the back of their hawker card. Cards are then separated into commissary locations.**

During this time, if vendors get to work early, they have a few choices: sit in the stands and shoot the bull with other vendors, find an asbestos-free place to sack out or relax, or slink into a corner somewhere and read the local paper, a good book or a girlie mag. Many vendors walk around with fancy earbuds, listening to their iPods or awaiting important phone calls from their homeys or from their wives reminding them to pick up milk on the way home. And there's the requisite poker game. (There's no worry for the players as management wouldn't dare go near the locker rooms what with the falling asbestos or the prevalent stink.)

Like any workplace, a fair share of gossip makes the rounds from the vendors. "Hey, you hear what happened again with Lazarus? This time he got caught asking some fan in the front row if he could get by him rather than walk all the way around to the next aisle! The nerve of that guy. Yeah, Jean will probably get another letter. He's gonna ruin it for all of us!"

"Yeah, like he almost did with the peanuts."

Technically, you're not supposed to be throwing things to the fans, like bags of peanuts. But who doesn't? One day back in the 1980s, I was selling peanuts in the upper deck when a woman stood up and signaled for a bag of peanuts and I threw them to her. She tried to catch it but she had these long *Guinness Book of World Records* nails and the bag slit open when she caught it. The peanuts went everywhere: in some guy's beer, on a bald man's scalp, and into some kid's ice cream cup. From then on, management instituted the Lazarus Rule:

NO MORE TOSSING YOUR NUTS!

Vendors will talk about how many beers or hot dogs or reheated pretzels they sold the night before or what they might expect that night or through the rest of the homestand. They'll comment on some of the babes in halter tops that walk by— *Yo yo yo check that out!*—or just chill out until call time. Sometimes a vendor might even watch batting practice and, if they're really unlucky, catch a ball with their nephew.

7. At a specified time, management will report to the product call area where all vendors will be waiting. Vendors will be told what product they are selling and from what commissary they are working.

Twenty years ago, management made product call in the bleachers and a crowd of vendors would wait breathlessly to find out what they were selling. The supervisor would stand on one of the rows of metal bleachers and try to talk above the din of the crowd, the howl of the public address system, and straggling fans. The supervisor would simply read off a long list of names that many couldn't even hear so they had to corner him after and ask him what they were selling and where they were selling it. Soon after call you would see a mixture of smiling faces, nonplussed and sad ones, and even a few perplexed ones milling about. Then came the usual: "How the hell did I get peanuts in the upper deck again?" "Aw shit! I hate selling Twizzlers!" "Yes! Hot dogs! I finally got hot dogs in the field!"

Then the call area was changed to inside the bowels of the stadium, just outside the vendors' locker room in the space big enough for the two VWs but taken up by scores of unused carts and scorecard stands. Once again, you could hardly hear the supervisor despite their screaming out your names, and once again vendors had to track him down just trying to find out what they had. Meanwhile, other vendors headed to the commissaries and got the jump on selling in the stands before some vendors even got there.

For years I didn't understand it. Why didn't they just post a staffing sheet on the wall where the vendors could find everything in one fell swoop? I never said anything for fear of a negative reaction. "Look, Lazarus, this is the way we run things here," The Penguin probably would've said. "Go start your own major league team and run the vending your way if it bothers you."

Finally, about two years ago, some genius decided that *you know what*, let's put up a sheet that shows what the vendors are selling and where they're selling it. (There are three vending stations on the lower level, one in the loge, four in the upper deck, and one in the bleachers.)

If you've ever been in a park and watched what happens when some kind soul drops breadcrumbs on the ground and saw how quick pigeons flocked to that spot, you've got a good idea at what it looks like when a hundred guys try to look at one sheet that's placed behind a locked glass case on the wall—as if it was the Mona Lisa at the Louvre.

Birds of a feather flock together

Yo yo yo, look and see what yur selling and get outta the fuckin way! Rusty, tell me what I got, I ain't got my glasses wid me. Holmes, what you got man?

There's pushing and shoving and grabbing and jockeying for position. It's sheer chaos as everyone tries to get a peek at this one little sheet.

Okay, who grabbed my ass?

Um, Jean, do you think you could post a *bunch* of sheets in the area?

8. After the staffing sheet is posted, vendors then proceed to the Money Room to get a proper price badge and change to work with. NOTE: Vendors are required to bring $50.00 with them to work each event in order to make change.

I can't tell you how many times that I'd go to get change and there wouldn't be any fives or tens or…old bills.

One thing I hate more than anything? New bills. Vendors need lots of singles and there's always an overabundance of brand new razor-sharp dollar bills. The problem is that when you're trying to make quick change—and an even quicker exit after telling a fan a joke that they just don't get, you want to give them their change in a hurry (if you give them any at all, according to The Penguin) and you don't want to peel off each dollar bill like it's a bra strap. If you do it in a hurry, you end up getting these little cuts on your fingers that you don't even realize at the time. But when you take a shower at home, *Ouch!* That stings!

9. Vendors then report to their assigned territory where the checker already has the hawker's card. Vendors receive their first load one half hour before game time and go out and sell. The checker marks down the load on the vendor's card. It is the vendor's responsibility to make sure the

checker has marked you down for your load. No vendor is permitted to visit another commissary in which they are not assigned to during the game.

Most of the time, one of the vendors working in the commissary will bring the cards for all the vendors in that station. There was one time that the cards didn't show up until nearly game time and the vendors were in a supreme panic. Finally the guy appeared with the cards. *Where were you?* asked the vendors. "Man, I had to go to the bathroom. *Bad!*" Talk about wanting to kill a man.

And then it's just about time to go out and sell sell sell. In each commissary, there are a number of porters that distribute the various food items to the vendors. After I established some seniority, I was the Hot Dog Man for a long time. The porter would take the dogs out of the freezer, empty them into a big vat of boiling water and let them cook—well, most of the time. Then he dumped them into my antiquated metal bin (the same one that's still used) which is full of water that's there for the whole game. That's where the term "dirty water dogs" comes from.

Now I sell beer. I pick up my tray full of warm beer that's encased in ice because the freezers are broken, and I'm ready to go. Well, not true exactly. After years of complaining, begging and beseeching by the vendors to fix the freezers, the beer has been pretty cold since the story broke in the *Daily News* in 2006 that the beer wasn't quite as advertised.

"If you want to get your cold beer at Yankee Stadium, you might want to bring your own ice pack," began the article.

The *Daily News* reporter was even armed with a thermometer and gauged the beer to be 60° on a day where temperatures soared into the mid-nineties.

(The new Stadium should have working freezers.)

"Lazarus, going out on one," I say. The checker circles the #1 next to my name and I'm off!

Like any other "highly skilled" profession, there's a method to what works and what doesn't. A good vendor combines stamina, speed, agility, intelligence and, in my case, a great sense of humor. (Plus, you work a lot faster when you don't give back change.)

Today, I'm on the third-base side. My boundaries are from the dugout to the outfield. I scout around to see where the other vendors are and I try to go to a place where they're not. Seems like common sense, but you'd be surprised. I'll pick an aisle where no vendor's gone up. I'll go up and down an aisle where other vendors would just vend in front of them, and I'll basically run around like a chicken with its head cut off for the next three hours: the Man in Constant Motion, yelling, "*Hey, Beer Man! Hey Beer. Man here!*"

I walk back towards the commissary when I see I only have a few beers left. Some vendors *must* be finished with their whole tray—no one knows why!—before they'll return to the commissary. That, of course, is an advantage for me. Hopefully each day I establish some bonds with customers. "Don't forget to come back in the third inning!" And that also adds to sales. Today I was lucky enough to do it with a half-dozen out-of-towners, all dressed in Cincinnati red. "Let me guess," I told them donning my best Thinker's pose. "Um, you guys are f-from …" They smiled. Then the midwesterners bought their drafts and tipped me handsomely.

Sometimes a funny or a kind word can make or break an extra beer sold now or later, or add to your tip. A tousle of a young fan's hair as you tell him, "Don't try to sneak in a sip" or "Pass this down, Champ," can do it. I schmooze with the fans a lot, but, admittedly, I'm no Cousin Brewski.

Sometimes someone waaaay down an aisle will order beer and it goes through a Conga Line to get there, the money and beer passing each other like two ships in the night. I've seen beer splatter, money fall and get lost, people jokingly pocket the money, and even people return money to a fan because they didn't realize the extra money was *my tip*.

In my younger days, I even saw someone take a bite out of some guy's hot dog and a fight almost ensued. The joker then bought the entire row franks. No tip, of course.

The best is when someone just *has* to find the exact change rather than break another bill. Here I am trying to Beat the Clock and this nut is looking for a quarter after giving me the dollars for the beer piecemeal.

"Hold on, hold on…I have it somewhere!"

Meanwhile, the fan doesn't realize it, but the people behind him are getting the shotgun ready because not only is he blocking the view but the stupid vendor is too!

"Excuse me," one woman once said as I waited for beer money. "But I came to see Jeter's ass, not yours!"

Some fans, when they see me laboring to get up the steps or notice my elbow brace or the sweat streaming down my face like I just emerged from a sauna, will ask me if the tray is "heavy." I tell them I'm used to it.

Being the Beer Man is like being a big breasted woman.
I've always got the straps digging into my shoulders,
my back is always killing me, and all the guys stare at my cups.

I constantly walk up and down the aisles, never going more than a few without yelling *Beer Here!* at the top of my lungs. Admittedly, my standard beer call is pretty generic but there are some vendors who have their own slogans to try and perk up sales, some better than others. Some will emphasize the brand most—Budweiser is the leader—some the fact that their beer is on ice. For last call, one vendor will cry "*Last call for beer, you alcoholics!*" There's one guy who doesn't understand why he doesn't sell that much. Maybe he needs to work on his slogan. "Hey beer here, get it while it's hot!"

After each tray is sold you come in and pay for your load, count your money (from the confines of the giant walk-in freezer if you're really hot!), take a brief sponge bath, towel off, yell your name upon leaving— "Laz goin' out on two!" and repeat seven, eight, nine and sometimes

12–15 times a day if the Red Sox are in town.

I wear out two, three pairs of New Balance sneakers a year walking the lower seats. There are boundaries for the vendors from different commissaries, and it's a rule of thumb not to break them. But you know the deal: in search of that extra buck, we all sometimes do.

10. **After the vendor sells his/her first load, that vendor returns to the commissary and pays the bank clerk their load. The bank clerk initials the vendor card as paid and the vendor takes out the next load. Only one load may be paid for at a time. No exceptions!!! This procedure continues until the bottom of the eighth inning. No vendor will be permitted to leave before the bottom of the eighth inning, unless for an emergency. Anyone who does check out before the bottom of the eighth inning will be subject to suspension and/or termination.**

Eighth inning? Unless some guy's pitching a no hitter or it's a playoff game, or I'm meeting Derek and A-Rod after the game for a few cold ones, I'm outta there! And besides, beer sales are cut off in the seventh and hardly anyone, save the ice cream man, works that late. Ice cream is, after all, more of a dessert.

The Yankees lost the opening game of this interleague series, the first meeting between the Yankees and Reds at the Stadium since the 1976 World Series, which was swept by the Reds in four games. (I wonder if Pete Rose bet the series.)

Has it really been over thirty years since I started working here?

Was beer really $1.15 back then? Or hot dogs seventy-five cents? Or water *free?*

Prior to today's afternoon game, Julia Ruth Stevens, the 91-year-old daughter of The Bambino, presented Alex Rodriguez with the 2007 Babe Ruth Award given to the player with the most home runs. A-Rod had 54, including # 500, which I watched sail gracefully over the left field stands, just inside the foul pole. I had to watch his every at-bat for something like three weeks until he finally hit his historic homer because every time he got up, so did the fans. You can't buy from me if you can't see me.

One of the perks of the job is seeing history made—and A-Rod's shot was pretty special.

Today's under-.500 Reds' team features future Hall of Famer Ken Griffey, Jr. He recently hit his 600th homerun to join a group of elite sluggers; for most New York fans this is their first time seeing the one-time prodigy. I watched him launch balls deep into the right field stands in batting practice as easily as swatting away flies at a family picnic and wondered how many he would've hit had he not been injured in his career. (I also wonder if he's steroid-free.) Griffey swings his Louisville Slugger, connects, and the ball rockets off the bat as if it's spring-loaded. He does it with such consummate ease, a la Alex Rodriguez, undoubtedly the greatest homerun hitter I've ever seen. I find it hard to believe that his dad, Ken Griffey, Sr., played for the Yankees from 1982–86, when I was still clamoring to work downstairs and not having to worry that every step in the treacherous upper deck might just be my last.

On this day, Griffey (who later in the season would be traded to the Chicago White Sox) would get a pair of hard hit singles and raise his average to .248. Hey, he's old and probably needed a dab of Biofreeze after the game.

When the Yankees are winning, most food items will sell better; it makes perfect sense when you think about it. With beer, when the Yankees are on top, the beer flows that much more easily. Fans cheer, their voices get parched, *Beer please!* When the team is losing, but it's a close score, beer sales aren't really affected—especially in the early innings. People come to the Stadium to eat, drink, and be merry so that's part of what they do. When the Yankees are getting blown out, people, as the vendors' say, "are sitting on their hands."

You don't use up a lot of energy listening to the loudmouth in front of you telling us how much the "Yankees Suck!"

After all, who wants to celebrate with a few brews on the losing side of an 8-1 score? But if there's a legitimate comeback in the making…

Beer man, over here!

Going into the series, the Yankees had been treading water at just above the .500 mark. A 4-2 loss in the opener has the $200 million dollar team searching for a truckload of answers to a season that's seen many of their players landing on the disabled list with alarming regularity and an uphill struggle seemingly from Day One.

Going into the sixth inning, pitching is dominating on both sides and the score is 0–0. The weather is comfortable enough to work—75º and cloudy—so I'm moving along at a fairly brisk clip without many pit stops to catch my breath. The fans try to start a fifth-inning rally as they're egged on by blaring noise from the loudspeakers and blinking scoreboard antics—**MAKE SOME NOISE!!! LOUDER! LOUDER!! LOUDER!!!** The Yankee bats, however, remain silent.

For $100, fans can get their name in lights on the Yankee Stadium Diamond Vision screen in center field. Things like birthdays, retirements, welcomes and an array of messages can make you a star for a stint. They've become as much a tradition at the Stadium as Kate Smith, the Bleacher Creatures, and the I'm-gonna-find-my-seat-on-my-own because the Yankees fired 99% of the ushers in 2000. Back then, a lawyer for the ushers said he was told by the Yankees that they needed the money to pay the salaries of the players. Back then, ushers made $72 a game and the Yankees payroll was *only* $92.5 million.

Beer is selling at a decent enough rate: I've sold six trays so far (144 beers) and have only banged three people in the head with my bin. (My season average is four.) A few fellow beer vendors have packed it in by the fifth inning, so that's always a plus.

In the seventh inning, the Reds score four runs to take the lead, my *LAST CALL FOR BEER!* doesn't go as well as it should because of that, and I call it a day.

I am beat and the Yankees are beaten up. They lose 6-0. Later on, I find that Derek and A-Rod have left a couple of messages on my cell to tell me they're not in the mood to meet for dinner, which is fine since I have a comedy show to do anyway.

11. **After the vendor is finished for the game, he/she will pay the banker for the final load. The checker and the vendor will sign the hawker card. The vendor takes the white sheet as a receipt and the checker brings the cards to the Accounting Department.**

I wash out my hat in the big commissary sink and drench my head under a glorious jet of water. Dripping wet, I pay the checker for my final tray of beer, give the porters "subway" (a tip, as it's known in vend-speak), and take my receipt to verify that I, Steven Louis Lazarus, was actually here on this day. I fold up the receipt and put it in my sweaty apron pocket as I catch my breath and walk out of the station.

For the day, I sold eight trays of beer at $204.00 a tray ($8.50 per beer), bringing in $1632.00 for the company and earning $301.92 in commission.

In my thirty years of vending at Yankee Stadium, I estimate I've brought in $2.5 million for the company, cash.

The least they could do is fix the leaky pipe outside the vendors' locker room, so I don't break my neck on my way to the back-end of the greatest double-play combination in the world.

12. **After you finish working, you must return the blue smock and white pants back to the Laundry Room attendant. Laundry bins are provided and dirty laundry is to be put in them. Any employee seen throwing dirty uniforms on the floor will receive a written warning and disciplinary action will be taken. Any employee not returning the uniform or seen leaving the building with the uniform will be terminated.**

I do my own laundry so I don't add to the mountain of clothes left on the locker room floor. Besides, I'd never get back my 36's if I did. I then proceed to reverse all I did at the start of the day. I take off my knee and elbow pads, escape from my wet clothes, put on fresh clothes which soon turn wet in the airless confines of the locker room, take a couple of more pills, spray my neck with more Biofreeze, and take another breath. I then fill out a card in advance for the Sunday, June 22nd game.

I would've loved to have taken a shower and walked out of the Stadium feeling refreshed and normal, not feeling like I had just walked through a giant puddle (which I had, actually, when I left). But instead, I shot the shit with a few vendors and was outta there.

I limped like an old man—a very old man—to my car and started thinking about the second half of my day-night doubleheader.

* * *

Working at Yankee Stadium and doing comedy, you put up with a lot in paying your dues. In comedy, you work your way up by doing open mics, coffee houses, dive bars or being an MC. You do a lot of things for free: benefits and parties and Sunday night shows where the only other people watching might be comedians. But you need to get your stage time so that's what we do. At Yankee Stadium, it was the same thing: I worked games at the start where I made twelve bucks, and I sold ice cream in April or soda when it was snowing or really crappy weather. But I stuck it out and sucked it up.

Now in both jobs, I'm a veteran. I had to hang in there, be persistent, and there were times I got disgusted, but it's all about not giving in and persevering and eventually, though it may sound like a cliché—heck, it *is* a cliché!—you move up the ranks if you have a modicum of talent, work hard, and get a few breaks. In comedy, you need one *big* break. I deal with the highs and the lows of both jobs because I'm blessed with two dream jobs.

Now I'm working in the box seats all the time. I have worked in nine World Series. How many vendors are lucky enough to do that? As a comedian, I've done stand-up in Las Vegas. How many comics are lucky enough to do that? And just how many people are lucky to do both?

To this date, I haven't met anyone with a similar dual career.

While it took me a decade to reach the top and finally sell beer, it took just four years to work at the Riviera in Las Vegas. Since vending is a commission job, it would pay to sell the highest priced product. Working in Vegas pays more than anywhere else and I've now reached the top at both jobs.

The next level up comes when *Hey Hotdog!* debuts on TV.

I wish I could say it was talent alone that got me to Las Vegas, but this ain't baseball where a guy can throw a hundred miles per hour with pinpoint accuracy and control and is noticed in an instant. There are only a limited amount in the world like him. In the stand-up world there are a zillion comedians and you usually need a little luck to break out of the pack. Funny isn't the only way you get there.

Yes, it could be your outstanding talent. In reality, it was probably something else.

Like who you know.

One night in 1999, I emceed for the hilarious Wendy Liebman at Governor's and she tried out some new material that just didn't work. Afterwards, I started thinking about a few possible jokes that might work for her to replace the ones that didn't. At first I didn't know if I could approach her as you hear all the time about headliners being "stuck up" and unapproachable, but she was really nice and down to earth. When I gave her some ideas, she said, "Oh sure, Steve, I'll try them, thanks!"

And they worked!

Wendy even ended up using a couple of the jokes on the *Late Show with David Letterman*. She was so thankful that she wanted to pay me for them. "Don't be ridiculous," I said. To "repay me" she was going to get me into Vegas. Uh huh, yeah, sure, right, I thought. I just took solace in the fact that I could help a fellow comedian. (Little old altruistic Stevie.)

A week later I was stunned when Steve Schirripa (who went on to fame as Bobby Baccalieri on *The Sopranos*) called to book me at the Riviera—and I've been performing there ever since. I always dreamed of doing Vegas and here I was.

I took a cab from the airport and as we approached the Riviera, I told the cabbie that I was performing there. "That's great," he said, half-

THE POPE AND ME AT YANKEE STADIUM

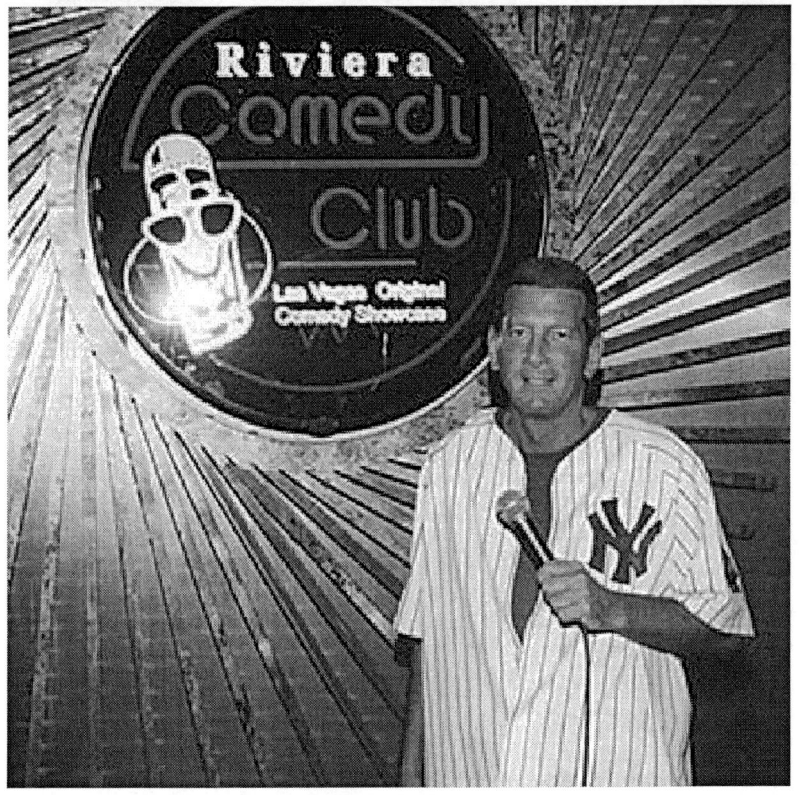

heartedly. "It's just around the corner." Seeing my name in lights up on the Riviera billboard, I screamed out, "That's me!"

The cabbie smiled and didn't say much. I gave him a nice tip anyway. Honestly, as much as I'd like to tell you everything that went on that first time in Vegas, I was simply too taken aback to even know I was there. I kept telling myself to make like it was just another club, but it was nearly impossible. What I remember most besides the butterflies and the applause and the friendliness of the crowds and the fact that they treated me like royalty and that my act went over well in a "foreign" land, was that almost every night before I went to bed I kept thinking about how I wish my mother was here to see me.

As Wendy Liebman says, "Envisioning the future helps create it."
About stand-up, she also said, "Pray that no one throws anything at your head."

Now they have penny slot machines in Vegas.
How sad is your gambling career if you're playing those machines?
I actually overheard some guy say to his wife,
'Honey I'm feeling lucky today! Go get me change of a nickel.'

I got in my car about 4:05 p.m. and immediately put the air conditioning in my Honda on full, feeling a blast furnace of hot air before the intoxicating cold air took over. I wiggled out of my spot and immediately called Peter Bales, who I would be working with in a two-man show at Reichart's Mardi Gras Restaurant in Danville, Pennsylvania. The show was at 9:00 p.m. We'd gotten the gig after the owner saw both of us perform in a Stand-Up University Graduation Show at the Brokerage Comedy Club on Long Island in March. We'd get five-hundred each.

"Do me a favor," I told Peter. "Call me around five-fifteen just to make sure I'm up."

"No problem," he said. "You can sleep in the car if you want. Just make sure you're awake for the tolls."

Peter has appeared as a stand-up comedian at comedy clubs, corporate functions and colleges across the country for the better part of three decades. He's appeared on FOX, A&E, Comedy Central, Lifetime, MTV, VH-1 and on Satellite Radio. For a while he hosted radio programs on WABC and WEVD in New York. In the 1980's he studied at Chicago's famous "Second City" and in the eighties directed The Laughter Company, an improvisational comedy group that helped launch the careers of Rosie O'Donnell and Bob Nelson. (They're not working in any restaurants tonight.)

As Peter knows, making it in this business is one part talent but mostly it's an inordinate amount of luck.

Normally, David Letterman *never* watches comedians perform on *The Late Show* but on one fateful day in 1995, he did. That comedian was Ray Romano. As you know, he became an "overnight" sensation. It took Ray 17 years to be an overnight success, or maybe *he'd* be driving me to Danville.

By the time I get home and take a shower, I'm fully exhausted and just want to lie on my bed forever, but there I am an hour later getting ready without the aid of Peter's phone call. I take three more Advil, spray the Biofreeze on my neck once again, and cram even more lozenges into my pocket. (I always worry about losing my voice.)

I stash my gear in Peter's car at 5:30 p.m. and *thank God* he's driving!

I have my microphone, should theirs not work, my tape recorder (as I always like to listen to all the silly mistakes I made!) and, of course, my 8 x 10 glossies because so many fans will be clamoring for one following my knockout performance. That is if I'm not too knocked out to perform.

Just a short way into the 150-mile trip, my stomach reminds me that I haven't eaten all day so we hit a service area somewhere off the Jersey Turnpike. I order a whopper at Burger King. "I went to a Burger King in Canada," said Ray Romano in his 1995 *Late Show* appearance. "You have to be bilingual to work there. In New York, they can barely speak *one* language. I had to *draw* them a picture of a hamburger."

I spoke with Peter and we decided that I would go on first since I was so tired. Peter would close the show. I'd do about a half-hour and Peter 45 minutes. Thinking about what lay ahead, I started to get nervous. No matter how many times I've performed, no matter how confident I might be that my act will do well, I always get nervous, be it at a dive bar, in Vegas, the Borgata at Atlantic City, or a church in Bayside.

I told Peter what jokes I would probably start with and he offered his opinion. In clubs outside of New York, I often worry about how some of my jokes will play out. I think should I use this joke or that one, or should I mention that I even work for the Yankees or should I open with my Jewish jokes or my New York jokes or a stock joke. A stock joke is one that comedians have used in some semblance of way, shape and form forever.

Later that night I'd use a stock joke in my opening: "My agent called and offered me a job for tonight. He said I could get you Trump's at Atlantic City in front of a sold-out house for big money opening up for Garth Brooks." I said, "Nah, book me at the Mardi Gras in Danville with about 50 drunken slobs and Aunt Ida celebrating her wedding anniversary."

"Just do your act," Peter tells me. "Funny is funny."

Like many comedians, Peter has a standard opening he uses whether at Dangerfield's in Manhattan, Harrah's in Atlantic City, or Bullfrogs Live Comedy Club in Topeka, Kansas.

"Hi, my name is Peter Bales. I want you all to remember my name. Spelled B-A-L-E-S. I hated that when I was a kid, because my nickname would be 'Balls.' I thought when I was older, I was done with that. But to this day, whenever I go to a restaurant I still hear, 'Balls, party of two. *Two* Balls.' Now I have to walk to the podium. 'Hi, I'm Balls. This is my wife Hooters.'"

As miles of highway unwind like black ribbons, the conversation ultimately leads to comedy. My sleep turns out to be a series of quick nods. Peter, a father of two teenagers who are often fodder for his act, lives with his girlfriend of 14 years, Peaches, who is also a comedian. Often they'll support each other. Once in a while they'll each say something funny.

Peter and I got around to talking about our current Stand-Up U class and some of the students in it. Inevitably, the conversation always turned for a little while into when we first started out, as we relived that just about every time we met with our students.

One of the students, Brad, was like a number of younger students we've had in the past. A bit brash and cocky, Brad early on decided that all of his jokes would be "shit" and "dick" and "fart" and "jerking off" jokes.

Stock joke #12: "So my dad walked in my room and caught me playing with myself. He said, 'Son, you know if you keep doing that you'll go blind.'

I said, 'Dad, I'm over here.'"

At Stand-Up U, we constantly preach staying "clean" because a dirty comic limits the places where he can work. Would Brad get laughs with some of his jokes? Sure, but most of the time it was that nervous type of laughter from the shock of hearing those particular words spoken aloud. A dirty comic doesn't have a long shelf life, sort of like bread left out on the kitchen table.

After all, there's only one Andrew Dice Clay.

We tried to tell this to Brad on a number of occasions but who can tell a 22-year-old anything?

Recently, I did a show at a Christian Coffee House called "Li'l Bit of Heaven" in East Northport, New York. The owner told me that there was to be no mention of sex or drugs or even an intimation of "shit" and "dick" and "fart" jokes. Just stay totally clean. No race or religious jokes or anything risqué.

I took it as a challenge because I knew that in my normal nightclub act, there are no holds barred. After all, they expect comedians to be somewhat dirty and there are rarely any restrictions. Plus, I wanted to do it because if I ever made it on television, I would have to be totally clean.

Also, here was a chance to do a freebie and give back a little for the breaks I've gotten. When I mentioned this scenario to Brad, he said, "Fuck it, I won't work shit like that." I realized how stupid he sounded as a comedian first starting out in the business.

Though it was hard for me, I did pretty well at "Li'l Bit of Heaven" and I was surprised a week later when I received a $50 check with a little yellow sticky note attached to it.

> STEVE, WE PASSED AROUND THE HAT AFTER YOU LEFT
> THEY LOVED YOU. THANKS SO MUCH FOR A GREAT JOB!

Peter and I both held out some hope that maybe somewhere down the road Brad would get it.

Sonia, another student in our class, *did* get it. Like Chris Monty, one of our past success stories, Peter, Rich, and I all thought that, for a newcomer, the blonde ex-cop had that rare stage presence…and nice cleavage.

Presently we were working on shortening her jokes. "Set-up punch line, set-up punch line," we stressed. And she was working hard to do just that. She had a lot of jokes where she was the focus and that was key: she joked about a drug bust in Harlem that went awry, being stopped for speeding in a small town, and a stint as an undercover prostitute.

"I'm a retired New York City police officer and I was assigned to work undercover as a hooker. They asked me how I felt about it and I said, 'Great. I already have the wardrobe.'"

"Always write what you know and make yourself the star," is what we tell our students.

We tell them that it's one thing to be funny in front of your friends and family, and that it's easy to make people you know laugh at a picnic or at the diner or at Uncle Rico's house on Thanksgiving. On stage in front of complete strangers when your mother or brother or girlfriend isn't around to laugh is another story. (We also told our students that they were always funnier once their check cleared.)

Working in a place where you've never done comedy before can be a hit or miss thing, which is the case tonight.

Will the place be set up like we suggested? Three of the main ingredients of a successful show are sound, lighting, and a stage. (Not to mention funny comedians!) *Will they even have a stage? Will the lighting be sufficient or will it be two bouncers with glow-in-the-dark keychains? Will the people be behind an obstruction that distorts the sound or the audience be spread so far apart that they'd need two cups and a long string to hear us?*

Even if there are twelve people, poor lighting, and a sound system from Radio Shack, we'll do our best. And besides, you never know who's watching. Maybe David Letterman is on vacation in Danville.

Our directions brought us right to the door without a hitch and we had plenty of time to have a small bite to eat. In many places, in spite of being the so-called "talent," they'll charge the comics for food and drink. Here it wasn't a problem.

Sometimes as the opening act, it's hard, very hard, to warm up an audience. Maybe they're still eating or maybe they just came to satisfy a friend. Maybe they weren't into comedy clubs or maybe they just didn't like the way I looked or what I was wearing.

Who knows?

There was a crowd of about 60 people in the rather large windowless room, and the stage was set up in front of a lavishly colored mural of partiers reveling on Bourbon St.

The owner had bought a seven-dollar floodlight, one of those clip-on types, at Home Depot and clamped it on a wall. The 300-watt bulb was positioned at the back of the room and it was blinding. Rather than say anything that might sound embarrassing to the owner, I clammed up.

I opened with the stock joke about performing in Danville rather than Trump's and I got a small laugh to start off my 30-minute set. It took me a solid two years to get 5-7 minutes of solid jokes on stage; the rule of thumb is that you should be adding about five new minutes of jokes a year for every year you're in comedy.

I did a few Jewish jokes that didn't go over as well as they might in, say, New York. As a comedian, it's perfectly fine to jump back and forth with topics. You don't always have to have a natural segue.

I told a few jokes about my family, my father's gambling prowess, a recent trip to the dentist—*ever try talking with a mouthful of novocaine after leaving his office?*—and I did a few Yankee jokes.

"As a beer vendor, it's my job to recognize when you're drunk. Heck, I can't even recognize when *I'm* drunk. Usually I start to tell you some of my jokes. If you start laughing, I know you're drunk."

Yankee fans are the roughest fans in the country.
They don't give you a chance. 'You suck.' 'Get off the field!'
I'm like, c'mon! At least give him a chance
to finish singing the anthem.

"In the bottom of the fifth inning of every game, there's always some guy proposing on the scoreboard. MARY, JIM WANTS TO KNOW: WILL YOU MARRY ME? The next thing you hear is 55,000 fans yelling out ASSHOLE! HE'S AN ASSSS HOLLLE!

"You know what I'd like to see? Someone getting divorced on the scoreboard. 'JIM, Mary says, I'M TAKING THE HOUSE, CAR, KIDS, AND DOG. YOU CAN KEEP YOUR YANKEE TICKETS. I HOPE YOU AND YOUR BLONDE BIMBO CHOKE ON A BALLPARK FRANK.... THIS DIVORCE SPONSORED BY NATHAN'S'"

I told a few jokes about being single, checked my timer that I keep on the stool next to my bottled water, and my time was up.

I passed the baton dutifully to Peter and looked for a chair to collapse into. Peter Balls had a great set and afterwards he sold his American History book, HOW COME THEY ALWAYS HAD THE BATTLES IN NATIONAL PARKS? and I sold my HEY BEER MAN! hats and 8 x 10 glossies.

"I'll autograph the hats anyway you like," goes my pitch for cash: "Derek Jeter, A-Rod, Mickey Mantle, even Yankees suck. And half the proceeds from my sales goes to Charity, my favorite topless dancer."

At the end of the show, the owner, who also doubles as the cook, paid us and said he was very pleased by the audience reaction. I asked him if he watched the show. "No," he said. "But it sounded good from the kitchen."

On the road about an hour later, Peter and I discussed the show: what jokes worked, what didn't, the incident with the Home Depot bulb and then, like a light, I was out.

I woke up in front of my house in no time. It was nearly 2:30 a.m. and I had to be up in the morning to go to Yankee Stadium.

"Thanks for helping me drive home," said Peter.

SEVENTH INNING

All the wrong moves

You can observe a lot by watching.
- YOGI BERRA

A LONG TIME AGO, in a galaxy far far away, I walked into the spare bedroom in our Bronx Blvd. apartment—the "junk room" as my mom used to call it—and stopped dead in my tracks.

What the he—?

Stacked across, up and down, and diagonally, was a tic-tac-toe assemblage of mismatched items. All the stuff appeared to be new. There were tennis rackets and pots and pans, flowery posters and picture frames, cutlery and dinnerware sets, bath towels and accessories. They shared the cramped space with toaster ovens and portable radios, some boxed, some not. There were coffee pots and tea kettles, toaster ovens and electric can openers, blenders and irons.

There was everything but a *Star Wars* lightsaber.

Boxes of shoes and sneakers, including Hush Puppies and Penny Loafers, Pumas, Pro Keds and Converse rose like buildings on a city skyline. There were glasses and tumblers, salt and pepper shakers, cartons of Winstons and Marlboros and Virginia Slims. Many of the items had a Caldor's price sticker on them.

I went for the Sony Walkman when my brother Ira walked in.

I had a feeling I wasn't in Kansas anymore. His smirk said that the Wizard of Oz was in the house. Maybe he could tell me what this clinking, clanking, clattering collection of caliginous junk was for. He could and he would.

"Interested in making some money, Steven?" Ira asked.

"W-well," I said. "What do I have to do?"

Ira explained the gist of it—nothing too complicated—and I bought in without him twisting my arm.

Before the internet, before electronic impulses could send packets of vast amounts of data and information across high-speed cable lines in split-seconds, shop owners, cashiers, sales reps and the like had to use the telephone for big purchases to verify a credit card you used. (This was long before the Citibank identity theft commercials.) You might have to show a driver's license or some other form of identification before they'd believe it was you. There might be that skeptical *No way you're old enough to buy beer look!* when you presented a Master Charge card reading XAVIER RODRIGUEZ but if your purchase was under fifty bucks, most of the time all they did was look at a weeks-old list of stolen cards and take a perfunctory look at your driver's license. The cards had a few days of shelf life before it would appear on an updated list, so there were no worries as long as they didn't call the charge in.

And that's what Ira had done. Using stolen cards he'd purchased from who knows where, he gobbled up goods that sold for fifty bucks or less. Then he'd get suckers like me to return them at stores like Macy's, A & S, and stores that have gone the way of the dinosaur: Alexander's, E.J. Korvettes, Woolworths, Crazy Eddie, and Caldor. After the stuff was returned, Ira would throw me a few bucks.

It was pretty easy work, and basically no sweat.

One day back in the Spring of 1980, I wanted to return a pair of tennis rackets, toaster oven, iron, and a bunch of picture frames at the Caldor store in Yonkers. I had no receipt. (Back then, depending on the store and/or personnel, you didn't always need a receipt or have to show twelve forms of identification to return something.)

"Hi," I said to the young clerk. Ira had told me to always go to the youngest cashier because it was *assumed* that they were the newest or knew the least or just didn't care; you get the idea. His logic made sense. "I'm here to return some engagements gifts that my wife got."

"No problem," said the girl.

After a few minutes of processing, my eye peeled on the overhead clock as post-time for the first race at Yonkers loomed (where I'd meet Ira afterwards) and my heart beating just a bit more than usual, the clerk handed me $117 for the goods, and I was on my way.

But a funny thing happened on the way to the track.

I patted down my wad of bills, made my way outside, and the gig was up.

As I emerged from the double set of electronic doors, Sgt. Joe Friday, who must've had a dragnet set up, was radioed by his partner from inside the store. *That engagement party kid, the one with the big nose, is headed your way!*

The plainclothes store detective flashed his plastic badge and ushered me back inside. I was in one of those rooms that you're apt to find in an old detective movie. All that was missing was the lone overhead light bulb and the guy saying, *We have ways of makin' you talk.*

"Listen, son," said the man. "Some kid this morning tried to return a whole bunch of shit and he had the same story as you about the engagement party."

I'm gonna kill Ira, I thought.

In the end, I gave the man all the money back, he gave me a little advice about not being seen anywhere near the store, and let me go. It was that simple. He could've gone a lot further. But then again, who knows what would've happened to the money he took from me?

Of course, later on at the track, when I told Ira what had happened, he wanted none of it. But he *did* want the money. He said I was lying, that I had made the whole detective story up. "Stop joking around, Steven. Where's the money?" I told him again I wasn't joking around. I wasn't lying.

Do I seem like the kind of guy that would do that?

Unfortunately, I'd end up doing things like this again and again. Deep in debt, gambling slowly and surely sucking the life out of me on a daily basis, I got so desperate that I would end up using my *own* credit cards and personal checks illegally. Like most juvenile delinquents, I was cocky enough to think I'd never get caught with any of the moves I made.

My state of mind, and dire financial straights, led to many moves like this, one more creative than the next. The degenerate gambler often thinks "outside the box."

Back in 1980, Yonkers Raceway had FREE CLUBHOUSE ADMISSION coupons in the local paper. Every day me and my friend Mario* went to candy stores, newsstands, supermarkets, and any stores that sold papers, and bought all of them for a dime each. We'd cut out and sell the coupons for a dollar at the track (regular admission was three bucks) and pocket the difference. Every night you could find us in the track parking lot selling those coupons. Here we were going all over the place to get these coupons, only to lose our earnings soon after gambling. "Why don't we go to the place where they print the papers and see how many we can get there?" Mario wondered.

So that's what we did one day after we both went broke at the track. We drove up to the Westchester printing plant and were amazed when we saw bundles of wrapped newspapers tossed in one of the garbage bins. Mario opened the hatchback of his Datsun 280ZX and I stood knee-deep in the bin, tossing bundle after bundle of newspapers to him.

Soon, some guard started running towards us with his billyclub in hand, a flashlight sending frenetic beams of light along the walkway.

Can you imagine seeing something like this on *Cops?*

In a getaway scene more likely to be seen in an old vaudeville show, I piled into Mario's car as he peeled away with some of the newspapers flying out of the hatchback (which we couldn't close). We bounced off the sidewalk on the other side of the street making a quickie U-turn, the front of the car scraping bottom, and zipped the wrong way down a one-way street on our way outta there.

We ended up getting about 500 newspapers, spent hours cutting out the free coupons, sold them all in the track parking lot through the rest of the week, and we ended up broke as usual.

We lost all the coupon money but kept the memories.

In 1985, I took this one step further.

On closing day at Belmont Park, the track was giving away booklets with all kinds of free coupons for Saratoga, the upstate track where racing would be switching to for the summer. There were coupons for admission, parking, food and drink, and even one for a free Daily Double

His name has been changed to spare his mother.

bet. I went in and out of the track at least a couple of hundred times that day. There were about five different windows where you could walk into the track grandstand, and after seeing me come and go a bunch of times, the clerks started to give me funny looks.

I made a joke each time like, "I think I left my keys in my car." "I have to get my binoculars." "I'm going to print some money."

I was upstate for a month. Every day at Saratoga I sold my coupons in the parking lot. I made $10,000 that one summer, only to promptly deposit it on horses that were a tad too slow.

God giveth and God taketh away. But not for long.

In January 1981, the American Totalisator Company (AmTote) created a new kind of betting machine for racetracks allowing people to make multiple bets. Thereafter, all wagers could be condensed into a single ticket. Prior to that, bettors, if they, say, bet $20 to win on a horse, would get ten individual two-dollar tickets. The advantages of the new machines were obvious: less paper printed, less fuss and muss for the gamblers to keep track of everything.

Just as AmTote was coming up with new ways to make money, so was I.

The Sting
Yonkers Raceway, April 1981

The usual suspects were involved in our little scam: me and Mario.

We had waited patiently for a horse that was a "sure thing" to win and we thought we had finally found one. Payoff N was a classy New Zealand-bred horse with a ton of wild early speed that had made a name for himself on the local scene by running faster and faster times each week while trouncing his competition. A few weeks back he'd finally reached the Open Handicap Pace, a feature contest that pits the best horses at Yonkers against each other. Payoff N, although showing his customary early flash in his last three races, hadn't been able to hold his speed to the end, even though he finished respectably each time. On this night, his connections were eligible to race the horse against inferior rivals in a lower class, and that's what looked to make him a standout or a "lock," as they say in the trade. His unbridled speed and the weaker competition made Payoff N, the # 5 horse, an overwhelming 2-5 betting favorite ($2.80 for every two dollars wagered). At the track you can bet to win, place, or show (1st, 2nd, 3rd) and that was, as legendary radio announcer Paul Harvey would say, "the rest of the story."

The plan was that we were going to make a big show wager on Payoff N, which, in all likelihood, would return $2.10 for every two dollar bet. So if we bet $500 (250 two-dollar bets) and he finished at least third, we'd get back $525.00.

Granted, we weren't stealing the Hope Diamond. We weren't ripping off a society party where we'd enter the joint with our pearly whites glistening and six-shooters blazing and look to fill our bags with strings of pearls and Rolexes and diamond pinky rings. It was small scores that kept us going.

This was to be one of those.

And what better place to beat than the racetrack, a place that had ripped the heart out of a zillion people through the years and turned mild-mannered people into totally lunatic gamblers.

The plan was to bet $500 to show on Payoff N, hoping he'd finish no worse than third, but we did so with just a *hundred* bucks.

As post time neared and the horses were on the track going through their final warm-ups, I was on the betting line. Mario was on the same line a few people back yelling, *"Come on! Come on! Let's get moving up there! I wanna put my bet in! Let's go!!"* Of course you can imagine that lots of other people now chimed in, as people usually did when they thought they weren't going to get their bets in as race time neared. The eighty-year-old teller at the betting window seemed to get a little flustered.

I was trying to time my bet to just about a few seconds before the race went off and that's exactly what happened.

"The horses are on gate," said the track announcer.

"Give me five hundred to show on the five, please," I said.

I gently laid down thirty singles with a twenty-dollar bill on top of the stack, a total of fifty dollars. The old man punched in a few buttons, the AmTote ticket slid out smoothly making a small whir as it did, and I took the ticket and made sure the teller saw me put it in my breast pocket. Then I walked away as the teller began to count the money.

"They're off! Payoff N flies out to the early lead…"

As I walked out towards the grandstand, I heard all kinds of commotion from behind: "Get that guy! Get that guy! *That's him!*" A flutter of footsteps and excited voices were set in motion when the teller flicked on the "trouble sign" above his window. A red light started flashing as sounds of *Whoop! Whoop! Whoop!* filled the air. Within moments I was surrounded by three burly security guards. The panting white-haired teller arrived soon after, his wire-rimmed glasses all fogged up, his face in a lather like a spent horse. He wiped off his glasses with his handkerchief.

"That's the g-guy!" he said, gasping for breath. "That's the one that b-bet the five-hu-hundred!"

I looked at him with that typical New York *Who me?* look.

I then turned, looked at each of the guards and back at the teller. "What are you *talking* about?"

"Don't tell me," he said. "I know what you b-bet! You said 'give me five-hundred to show on the five horse,' but you only gave me fifty bucks. I saw you put the ticket in your shirt pocket!"

"I think you're losing it," I said quietly, composed as could be. "I only bet fifty!"

"All right, buddy, empty out your pockets," said one of the guards.

Meanwhile, I was watching one of the television sets that was mounted on the wall. Payoff N was steadily drawing away from the field with less than a quarter-mile remaining. *"Payoff N now leads the way by four lengths!"*

As Payoff N left the field in the dust, I was still surrounded by one angry teller and three armed guards. "All right fella, let's see the ticket," one of them said.

"I don't understand," I said quietly, watching as Payoff N crossed the finish line, the easiest of winners. My insides were smiling. "Why do I have to show you anything?"

"If you don't show us the ticket, it'll only make things worse."

Slowly, grudgingly, I took the ticket out of my shirt pocket and handed it to the teller. The old man's face went ashen as he looked at the ticket. He did a double-take and just stared at it, perplexed. It was that classic snapshot of disbelief, as if he'd encountered the boogey man. His mouth hung open, and his body went rigid. He was fixated on the ticket. The crowd that had built up around us stood silent.

Then he handed me back the ticket, the one that showed only fifty dollars to show on Payoff N, the five horse. "I d-don't understand," mumbled the old man, shaking his head. "He b-bet five-hundred to show! I know what he said. I d-don't get it…I know I punched out a five-hundred dollar ticket!" One of the guards looked at the ticket, then handed it back to me with a big *I don't get it* look.

I slowly walked to the window and cashed the original fifty-dollar show bet. The teller had to be thinking *What the fuck?*

Meanwhile, Mario was off in the clubhouse cashing the five-hundred dollar show ticket.

And now, *the rest of the story.*

Immediately after the betting windows opened for Payoff N's race, Mario had gone to the old man's window and bet fifty dollars to show on Payoff N. I took the fifty-dollar show ticket from Mario and I put it in my shirt pocket. When I took the five-hundred dollar ticket from the window later on, as Mario did his best to stir things up—*"Come on! Come on! Let's get moving up there! I wanna put my bet in! Let's go!!"*—I made sure the teller thought he saw me put the ticket in my shirt pocket. After I got the five-hundred dollar ticket, I simply passed it to Mario as I walked by him on line. He quickly made a bee-line for the clubhouse on the other side of the building. By the time I finished stalling the guards, before they insisted I show them the ticket, Mario had already cashed the five-hundred dollar ticket in the clubhouse. Payoff N, who finished first, paid $2.10 to show. We got back $525 on our investment of $50, and got back another $52.50 on the fifty dollars we put down to buy the original show ticket.

I don't recall, but I'm sure we blew the $477 in profit in no time.

* * *

"You see that girl sitting in the front row?" the comedian said. "I did her last week. She follows me everywhere."

I'd heard the claims before.

I had sex with this one. I did it with that one in the back room at Harrah's in Atlantic City and with that cute blonde over there on top of the lions' cage at Circus Circus. See that one standing near the pool table? I did her in the back seat of a limo on the way to a fundraiser for Girls Gone Wild.

After reading Wilt Chamberlain's 1991 book, *A View from Above*, and his claims of sleeping with 20,000 women, I realized that we both had a lot in common, though he's been dead for years: We both loved basketball and each of us had a good sense of humor.

Hard to believe with me being the chick magnet I am that I'm a mere 19,990 women behind Wilt.

I always loved the old-time comics. Comedians like Buddy Hackett, Jerry Lewis, Shecky Greene, and Alan King often performed in the Catskills, in upstate New York, near where my family and I stayed during the summer at Lansman's Bungalow Colony. My mom and dad ran the luncheonette at Lansman's (perfect for my dad with Monticello Raceway being just down the road), and I whiled away my time flipping baseball cards, going swimming, playing baseball, basketball, and paddleball and kid games like Ringelevio and Spin the Bottle.

In September 2000, when I got a chance to be inducted into the famous Friars Club in New York City, I was fortunate to meet many of those comedians that I envied, along with some of the biggest stars in the entertainment industry. Its members, past and present, reads like a *Who's Who* of Beautiful People.

Since then, I've been lucky enough to perform at the club when the Friars christened the first floor bar area as the BILLY CRYSTAL ROOM, when they honored sports stars—*roasted* them, actually—like Rusty Staub and David Cone, and celebrities Jerry Lewis, Don King, and Donald Trump.

During a break in the David Cone roast, I chatted with then Yankee manager Joe Torre. When Torre found out I was single, he put his arm around me and said, "Son, hang in there and keep plugging away. I batted .363 in 1971 but still struck out 70 times. Sometimes you're gonna

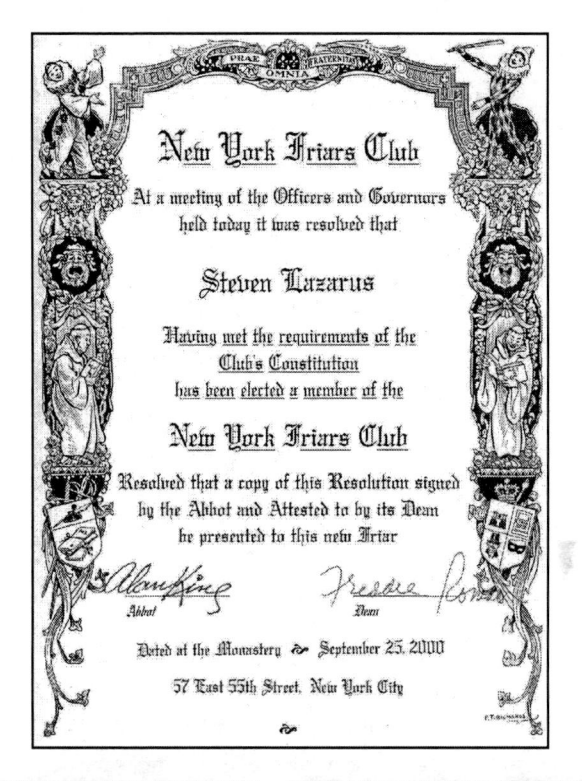

> **New York Friars Club**
>
> At a meeting of the Officers and Governors held today it was resolved that
>
> **Steven Lazarus**
>
> Having met the requirements of the Club's Constitution has been elected a member of the
>
> **New York Friars Club**
>
> Resolved that a copy of this Resolution signed by the Abbot and Attested to by its Dean be presented to this new Friar
>
> *Alan King*, Abbot   *Freddie Roman*, Dean
>
> Dated at the Monastery ~ September 25, 2000
> 57 East 55th Street, New York City

strike out with some women, and sometimes you'll connect."

Torre, of course, is right.

Then along came Mary. We'd hooked up through the on-line dating service Match.com and after going back and forth several times between emails and on the phone, we made arrangements to meet. You know women: it's gotta be where there's a lot of people, bright lighting, and a good atmosphere. My original suggestion of McDonald's didn't cut the mustard. She told me a place we could meet and I agreed. It was a downcast day but I was in a pretty good mood.

I didn't think the place would have any effect on our date. If Mary and I liked each other, or we couldn't stand each other, the place would have little bearing. Boy was I wrong!

Sterling Bowl had gone out of business in 2001, and Strike Long Island, a ten million dollar entertainment complex had been built in its place. The state-of-the-art "Adult Underground" featured glow-in-the-dark bowling in a swirl of psychedelic colors, an indoor go kart track, pinball and video machines, pool tables, a dance hall, and two wall-to-wall bars.

I'd bowled in a league at Sterling for ten years and I had some good times before the crash back to earth.

Mary and I were to meet at the bar.

The moment I got there I ordered a stiff drink as a floodgate of bad memories burst forth.

> I joined one of those on-line dating services
> so I upgraded to high-speed internet service.
> Now I get rejected by women a thousand times faster.

The Kings & Queens Bowling League had a feast fit for, well, kings and queens.

The usual staples for a year-end celebration were on the menu: overcooked hamburgers piled high like a mountain of discarded tires, a chorus line of hot dogs with jars of Gulden's Spicy Brown, trays of shrimp on shaved ice, generous portions of macaroni salad, potato salad and coleslaw, and the usual array of cold cuts. Not many people would end up eating the dessert.

Being secretary of the league for the last few years, I was entrusted to be treasurer, and tonight the league was there to split up the prize fund after 36 weeks of competition.

In 1992, a little more than a year after my mom died, and shortly after my Camaro flipped over on the Throggs Neck Bridge when some idiot in a major rush cut across three lanes, my direction in life had as much chance as a golf ball heading for a bunker. (Comedy was still three years off but for now mental and physical pain were ever present.)

And then the degeneracy really took hold.

When my mom died, I went off the deep end, gambling wise. I used up the little savings I had and maxed out the rest on my credit cards. When I learned about the ridiculous bankruptcy laws, and realized I had nothing that creditors could lay claim to if I didn't pay off my cards, I went nuts. I bought plane tickets to Vegas and started gambling there. I took out $1000 cash advances and bet that. I gambled in Atlantic City, made bets at Yonkers, called in sports bets with several bookies, and ate in the best steakhouses in town. For the moment, I was the newly crowned lottery winner.

"What's the worst that could happen?" I reasoned. By the time I'd reached $20,000 in debts, no one would honor my cards. Then I started using my own checks and they started bouncing.

Then it *really* got crazy.

I never thought I was the typical degenerate gambler. I just needed something to keep my interest, something to *do* as I got zero pleasure from my regular job. If I lost everything at the track or owed my bookie a huge sum, I'd simply keep taking out cash advances on my American Express or Master Charge and Visa cards.

When the credit cards ran dry, I had no money, not even enough to pay the rent. Then one day I thought: *I'm in charge of the bowling alley money!*

Oh boy.

Each week, bowlers paid $15 for their bowling and after Sterling Bowl got their cut, the rest would go into the prize fund to be distributed depending on how the teams finished. Every team got some kind of payoff. It was $500 per person for first, $350 for second and so on all the way down to the team in last place. There were 16 teams and four people on each team.

Little by little I started dipping into the prize fund. At first, I started with $500 bank withdrawals and when I lost that I took another $500. I knew sooner or later I'd make the money back and return it, but it didn't quite work out that way. I started chasing after the lost money with bigger and bigger bets. I started betting hopeless long shots at the track trying to catch lightning in a bottle. All I did, though, was get burned. I kept thinking, kept *hoping* that if just *one* of those long shots came in, I'd get all the bowling money back. I started making crazy sports bets where three teams would have to win and, though I'd score every once in a while, the debt grew larger while the window of opportunity (to put the money back) got smaller. By the time I knew it, there was no money left.

Poof! Fifteen thousand down the tubes.

In the past, friends had bailed me out of smaller jams, but this wasn't quite like that. This was a little more serious. Heck, this could mean *jail.* As the day to disperse the prize fund neared, I begged friends to help me out, but it wasn't happening. I don't know if they were taking a tough stance in order to teach me a lesson, didn't have the money, or simply weren't willing to trust me that I'd ever pay it back. (I lean to the latter.)

As a result of all the stress and anxiety, I lost 20 pounds and I hurt a lot of people. But mostly, I was scared. What would *I* do if I came into the bowling alley expecting money only to be told the treasurer of the league gambled it away? Would I want to beat the shit out of the guy? Would they? My league had entrusted me with their money, had bowled for nearly 10 months and now they'd be told, well, I would've had the money if the four horse in the fifth race at Belmont had my nose…

Finally, it was time to face the music.

*   *   *

```
http://webmail.aol.com/34032/aol/enus/mail/display/message.aspx
email from Kathy Roper, ex-girl friend Thursday, February 19,2008
My reaction to the bowling alley incident…wow! You were
perceived as arrogant in the league so I was so sur-
prised that you were going to humble yourself and meet
with the group. I was nervous, very nervous for you and
```

not sure why but for me, as well. At the time I felt like I should stand up and support you but I wasn't bold enough to. I think at the meeting a fair percentage of the league felt sorry for you. The other half was just mad they lost their money. I think it was hard for anyone to understand not so much how you could take money to gamble, but how you could do it to people who you saw every week.
If people have never been exposed to an issue like yours or were not close enough to you to understand the problem, it is even harder to grasp or have sympathy for. For me it was a very uncomfortable hour. I was also nervous that someone was going to say something to upset you and you would retort in a way that would fail to elicit sympathy but at the same time it was difficult to see you standing, so vulnerable, in front of the room. I was a bit naive at the time. I realized you gambled a bit much but didn't realize the extent of your problem. That's why I was so surprised when I heard the news. Mario really acted as a good friend should....

*   *   *

Mark, Mindy, Mario and my brother Berny were brave enough not only to drive me to the lanes but to stand by my side when I spoke to the people. My only plan was to look the people in the eye and tell them exactly what I had done.

Hi there! I just want you to know I robbed you guys of fifteen thousand dollars. Thanks and enjoy your dessert!

That might be the way it plays out on *The Pope and Me at Yankee Stadium* on Comedy Central. At Sterling Bowl, it was a tad more serious. After I spit out the truth in broken sentences, there was silence for a few seconds as some in the crowd didn't know what to think.

"You're joking, right Laz?"

No answer.

"What do you mean you *gambled* away the money? Where's the fucking money?"

Some people said nothing. Some stared in disbelief. Others came a bit closer. First my friends, then the league president, tried to stave off the cavalry with some soothing words as I tried to choke out how sorry I was but never really got the chance as things got loud.

I was told later that others thought I simply pocketed the money like I had Swiss bank accounts or off shore accounts to deposit them into. Had I been the one sitting there and the treasurer said things like that, I would've freaked out too. No one leaped to attack me but there were several heated exchanges where people in the league stepped in like good Samaritans at a traffic accident. I know I probably would've wanted the guy lynched. Take a noose and hang him from the tree in the center of town to show what happens when you fuck with the Kings and Queens Bowling League.

There were those that felt genuine sympathy for me, staring blankly and patting me on the shoulder, and there were those that vowed that they'd get their money, "you just wait and see."

All the other times I'd made moves, I beat the credit card companies or the racetrack or things where no individuals really got hurt or lost any money. Now it was my friends and family that suffered and I felt like the scum of the earth. I suffered many sleepless nights and became paranoid about going to jail, which I could never tell anyone because, honestly, who would care?

People were in tears because of what I'd done. They came there expecting their money and I never stopped to think about anyone but myself. Gambling can do that to you. I really wanted to get out of the bowling alley as quickly as I could and bring this bad reality show to an end, but I could see that wasn't going to happen until everybody had their shot at me.

And rightly so.

"He can't escape that easily!" cried someone. "He's gotta pay for what he did," said another shaking his fist at me. Only last week, I had food and drinks with these same people and now some of them would've loved to see me dead. I honestly didn't know what could happen, but a few days later I found out when two detectives came to my house to arrest me.

I'd finally hit rock bottom; this was my wake-up call. I later found out that the American Bowling Congress (ABC) had emergency insurance in case just such a thing happened and many people would get a portion back of what they lost. In the end, I was able to avoid any jail time by agreeing to pay back the $15,000, and I did so over a period of years.

I never did bowl in a league again, and I thought I was done making all the wrong moves.

A week later, my Mitsubishi Eclipse was stolen from in front of my house. It was never found.

* * *

I spoke few words to Mary in the half-hour we were at Strike. I nursed my drink and marveled at the incredible makeover that had turned a drab underground bowling alley into one of the hottest night spots on the Island. I thought, too, about the chain of events here 14 years ago and how my own life had been transformed because I was lucky enough to find comedy.

Where would I be without it? In jail? At the bottom of the East River in cement shoes? Working at Schulgheis & Panettieri doing ledgers? Yikes!

I reflected on how truly lucky I had been to find my niche in life, and thought about how so many people were miserable doing jobs that they hated.

We paid for the drinks, walked outside, and Mary and I quickly went our separate ways. In the interim, the sun had come out.

SEVENTH INNING STRETCH

God Bless the Beer Vendors,

Men that we love,

Get beside them, and guide them

Thru the night with your arms raised above.

Forget the Pepsi, and the ice cream,

I want a beer cup, filled with foam

God Bless the Beer Vendors,

While our runs come home

God Bless the Beer Vendors,

Wherever we roam.

EIGHTH INNING

The Road Taken
October 21, 2000

*Things could be worse.
Suppose your errors were counted and published
every day, like those of a baseball player?*

- ANONYMOUS

I WANTED TO KILL MYSELF. I thought I was past all this nonsense.

All I had to do was swallow a dozen or so Advils, shut the windows, start the car, assume the position and...

Wait. Don't I have to stick a banana in the exhaust pipe and be in an enclosed space? And didn't I put in to work tonight's playoff game?

I sensed a car pull alongside mine. I ignored it like any reputable New York driver does when they don't want to expend the energy to tell someone, "No! I'm not going out!"

Beep! Beeeep!

I dared not turn my head, knowing what I might find.

I know it's him, I told myself, I know. It. Is. Him. My reddened eyes and haggard WILL WORK FOR FOOD look made it obvious I wasn't ready for this. Can't I just go to sleep now and forever? I couldn't believe I had to face the music, despite my head being a drum roll of pain.

Reluctantly, I rolled my Honda's window down as eternal rest was momentarily put on hold. Unfortunately, the architect of another failed get-rich-quick scheme—a complete and utter disaster just the night before—was staring me in the face; at that moment, I'd rather have been looking down the barrel of a shotgun.

How many times had we pulled a Ralph Kramden-like stunt in lieu of the quick buck?

"Going out?" Mario asked, hooking a thumb at me. Same standard line we'd been swapping with each other for the last thirty years when one of us needed a parking spot near the Stadium, and the other already had one. "Whatcha doin?" he asked, as if my face wasn't a dead giveaway.

"I'm figuring out a way to kill myself," I said. "Got any bananas?"

Down the street, white-gloved cops with garish orange and yellow vests were pinwheels in motion trying to keep traffic moving, the area a beehive of activity. Swarms of stretch limos, chartered buses, SUVs and family sedans shared space parked on sidewalks and in disorderly zigzags on the dirt and grass, normally a makeshift area "reserved" for the locals for small family gatherings during the day or a toke or two at night. Tailgate parties were going full blast in the open-air parking lot just across from Yankee Stadium. Plumes of coal-black smoke filled the air, some from portable grills nestled in open car trunks and others precariously set up on spindly legs.

A state-of-the-art motor home, painted in bold blue-and-white pinstripes, a sign above the huge panoramic front windshield proclaiming "Yankee Clipper," was parked parallel to the Kinney Parking Lot. A pair of fans sat in lawn chairs sipping beverages and nibbling on cold cuts. A couple of cops patrolled the area.

All this just a long *A-Bomb from A-Rod!* away from the Stadium, as Yankee announcer John Sterling likes to say. Alongside the Major Deegan Expressway, news vans from local and national stations—FOX, ESPN, CNN, MSNBC—their coiled antennas stretched to the sky, were lined up like a marching band ready to beam pictures to eager viewers around the country for this second momentous night.

The festive mood did little for me.

Years later, Mario the brainiac would inform me: "You didn't look too good that day."

No shit.

OPERATION GRAMPRO had gone up in smoke like an exploding cigar. I was left holding the bag—literally—one that only 24 hours earlier had five-thousand dollars in it—*my entire savings*—and now lay empty in the passenger seat.

Just the mere mention of that time and I start breathing heavy. Yeah, they say it's easy to laugh after an extremely tough time in your life, but even to this day, it's hard, believe me. Could there have been anyone more miserable than me before Game 2 of the 2000 World Series between the New York Yankees and New York Metropolitans in the first Subway Series since 1956?

The city that never sleeps couldn't even take a nap the night before in what turned out to be a very long evening.

And neither could I. The seeds of desperation had been planted only a few days prior.

"Listen," came the 4:00 a.m. voice. It was Mario.

"Do I have to?" I said. "Can't you speak to me in the morning?"

"It is morning. Listen!" he insisted. "What's the one thing that you know everyone is gonna get when they go to the game?"

Some sleep?

Funny. I rubbed my eyes.

He paused, then blurted: A PROGRAM!

"Yeah…so?"

"Well, the only way you can possibly get one is if you're either at the game or someone gets one for you, right?"

Suddenly I could hear the noises that can make any house spooky between dusk and dawn, when stillness and quietness join forces. The slow, monotonous ticking of the battery-powered wall clock, the refrigerator humming, the cars on the Clearview Expressway, the gurgling of the water pipes trying to send up early morning heat, the beat of your heart…and I had an idea where this was leading. I sat up.

"Go on," I said.

I admit: Mario's spiel was convincing. So much so that I put together every penny I could muster so we could buy a *thousand* World Series programs in advance. Forget about working an instant big-cash game like Mets-Yankees on a Friday night, a Friday *beer* night for a World Series game. We were gonna buy programs and paint the town orange, white, and blue.

We knew it was easy math and easy money and the best thing was we could do it for every World Series game: pay ten bucks per program, sell 'em for twenty. *No one else could possibly have them…it's a can't lose proposition. Wouldn't you buy one if someone was selling them?*

The Pope and Me Director's Cut would eventually show close-ups of two Centerplate vendors: one calm, cool, and composed, the other one harried with sweat stains apparent under the armpits and in the middle of the long-sleeved navy blue company shirt. His brow furrowed, lips dry as the desert. Mario was the unflappable one. Me? A nervous wreck. I was now officially broke and jeopardizing my job to boot.

Oh yeah.

We were supposed to be selling these FALL CLASSIC keepsakes to the Stadium faithful before and after the game—and here we were on the streets of New York hawking our wares like fake Rolexes as first-pitch time neared at the crammed House that Ruth Built. Hard-to-believe I'd go through with this rather than selling beer during the game.

But I did.

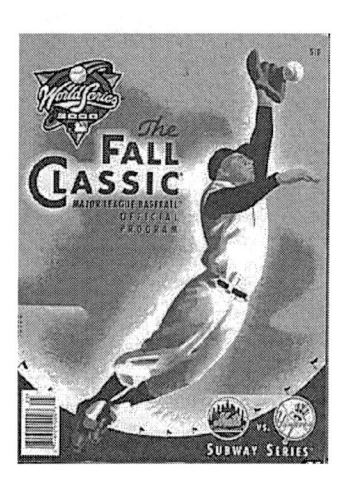

As we snaked the long hand truck through the corridors of the bustling Stadium—ever try to steer a shopping cart through a food aisle with wobbly front wheels?—the weight of the 40 boxes made a straight, easily accessible path to the Stadium exit an impossibility. Indeed, it appeared that a drunkard was at the helm. I remember boxes falling off the hand truck this way and that, and me, alias The Flash, darting to scoop them up, paranoid that fans would steal them. Except for a bar-coded white invoice that indicated each box had 50 programs in it, no fan could possibly know what was in those boxes, though my eyes darted everywhere as if each one read:

ATTENTION FANS
WORLD SERIES PROGRAMS IN THIS BOX

in dazzling Broadway-like neon signs.

While I seemed to take it all in slow motion, and worried as we moved in fits and starts, Mario had his eye on the prize. "We'll be fine, Steve, don't worry about it," he said as he we slogged our way through the quagmire. Mario was a juggernaut: "Excuse us! Coming through! Watch it please! Excuse us! Coming through! Watch it please!"

We wended past souvenir and concession stands (the other vendors giving us Barney Google eyes because they knew what was in the boxes but were puzzled nonetheless), yellow-shirted Burns Security Guards with walkie-talkies clipped to their shirt, STAFF written on their back in Yankee blue, and past Secret Service-like enforcers with dress-for-impress blue blazers and slacks and ear buds that lent them an authoritative air and were probably hooked up to George Steinbrenner's shoe phone. We wiggled past all those dazed and confused I-can't-believe-I'm-here-for-the-World-Series fans that couldn't find their seats even if they were in the Yankees dugout.

"Stop worrying…please?" Mario kept telling me. "We'll make it, *geez!*"

Sure, easy for him to say since he wasn't risking his life savings or his job, and his heart wasn't beating like a piston. This was to be Mario's last hurrah at the Stadium, and he couldn't give two shits if he was caught, though, I believed neither of us was doing anything wrong (well, I kept trying to convince myself, anyway). I mean we *had* paid for the programs in advance and far as I knew nothing in the union contract stipulated we couldn't buy some of the things we sold.

Once we made our Houdiniesque escape from the bowels of the Stadium, we encountered obstacles that had us duking and juking and zigging and zagging and stopping and starting and bumping and thumping and grinding and winding through and around a man-made hell, angry winds swirling around us as if the Baseball Gods were saying *Oh yeah? Ya wanna keep playing baseball into late October? Take that!*

I never stopped to think that there'd be even *more* people to contend with once in the clear, not to mention the fact that the car was parked a good half-mile away.

The charged atmosphere led to a spruced-up South Bronx oasis for the Subway Series, and a highly secure one at that. New York's Finest flexed their collective muscle with POLICE COMMAND CENTER battle stations set up in trailers on the Stadium's perimeters as choppers roared overhead and an army of flak-jacketed police, some in riot gear, some sitting ramrod-straight atop their mounted steeds, brought a dose of "calmness" to the scene. Elite members of the bomb squad walked their German Shepherds around like they were at an outdoor Westminster Kennel Club event, their vinyl K-9 windbreakers flapping like clothes on a line.

Not to be outdone, the Fire Department had huge Seagrave Pumper fire trucks from Engine Co. 68 and Ladder 49 at the ready, should anyone light a match or start a bonfire. Even the trucks were adorned in Yankee colors with the interlocking NY and Yankee logo stenciled on their sides.

Wasn't this supposed to be just a friendly baseball game between two boroughs?

There was the usual gaggle of fans and tourists, some with bags as big as American Tourister luggage, some noshing on hot pretzels or grilled franks, and others just gawking at the surroundings as game time neared. A group wearing Tino Martinez jerseys looked at the imposing grandeur of the home office for baseball and couldn't get enough of it.

"Yankee Stadium...*mucho grande!*"

They were oblivious to two guys and a hand truck as we forged past.

I watched a number ❹ train, the Lexington Avenue Express, en route from Woodlawn in the Bronx to Crown Heights in Brooklyn, rumble overhead. In the last post-season Subway Series back in '56 between the Yanks and the Brooklyn Dodgers, fans that couldn't get a ticket lined the elevated station above right field to get a glimpse of the game, something that had been going on for eons even for strap-hangers that were just waiting for the train. Thanks to the refurbishing of the Stadium back in 1975, that right field view was "Going, going, gone!" as Mel Allen, longtime voice of the Yankees used to say when a Bronx Bomber nailed one.

A flotilla of vehicles from Emergency Services Units, Police SWAT teams in armored trucks, city buses with stickers that read THIS IS A HYBRID VEHICLE, yellow taxis, passenger cars and gypsy cabs (really, is every one a battered Lincoln Continental?), clogged the arteries around the Stadium like trans fat.

And what was I thinking? I couldn't believe I was actually doing this. How can't I be inside selling beer? Am I losing my marbles? Like ballplayers living their dream, *this* is what vendors waited for: THE WORLD SERIES. The really big payday was here—and I was on the outside looking in.

The night before, Mario had said, "Steve, the money doesn't get any easier than this. How many people have already asked you to pick up a program for them?"

"Yeah, but walking out of the park with a thousand programs is a bit much, no?" I said.

"Hey, if someone questions what we're doing we'll just tell them we paid for the stuff already. *Don't we plan to?* And we'll show 'em the receipt. What's the problem?"

"Well...um, it's just that..."

"We'll just tell them our families wanted a bunch of Yankee programs."

"Yeah, right, they'll buy that," I said sarcastically.

"Okay, we'll tell them our *very big* families."

In the end, save for fellow vendors' questioning looks, no one had stopped us to ask what we were doing and, it seemed, no one really paid us any mind.

So why was Mario so emboldened? Whenever we'd made moves in the past, he was always the scaredy cat, he was always the one that was afraid of what might happen, he was always the one that had to be convinced not to worry.

Not this time.

Once upon a time, On August 21, 1999, an idea forty years in the making was hatched. That day, Mario, a long-time old car buff, was mindlessly searching around on eBay when he found the stuff that dreams are made of: a classic 1959 Cadillac Ambulance, like the one used in the movie Ghostbusters. Though it was up for sale, this one looked like it would've had a few problems transporting accident victims or removing ghosts from city buildings.

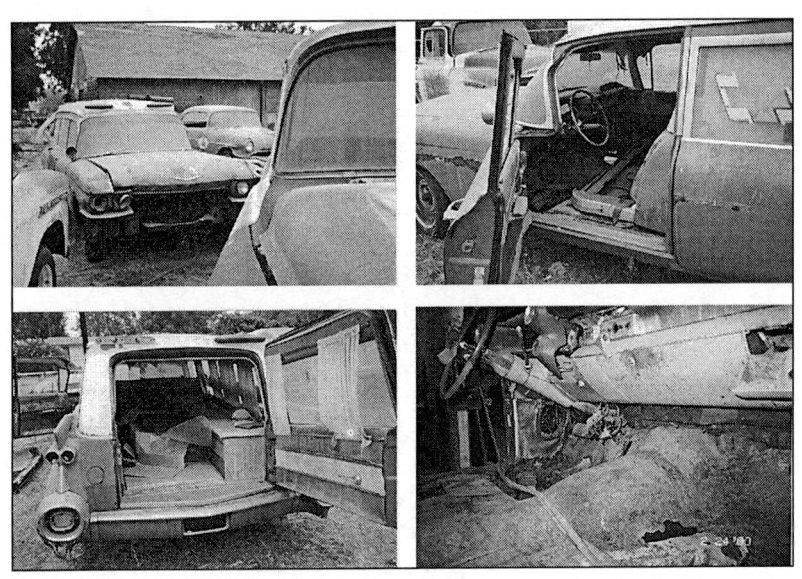

Instantaneously, Mario got the idea for a new kind of rolling billboard company. Within a few seconds, he came up with the name:

EMERGENCY ADVERTISING
The World's Most Unique Rolling Billboards

Everything else would take a wee bit longer. Of course, I went along for the ride.

> *"How did I know they were building a drive-in theatre?"*
> - Ralph Kramden's response when reminded by his pal, Ed Norton, of a business venture in which they bought land to build a parking lot for a new movie house being constructed across the street.

At the time, with the exploding use of the internet, some five thousand new companies were coming on-line per week. Obviously there was a need to get the word out quickly, or else. Mario intended to fill that need.

And, of course, he wanted to drag me along with him.

In those go-go days of the Wild West Internet Orgy, the frenzy for on-line gold created the need for In-Your-Face advertising. What better way to get instant exposure than a company advertising their goods or services using an eye-catching 1959 Cadillac ambulance with a giant billboard on its roof? Just the 42-inch tail fans would be enough to attract attention, especially if you got impaled on one of them. (Indeed this is what happened to many kids playing in the streets in days of yore.)

Customized billboard trucks had been around since the early 1990's. They had a monster-sized billboard attached to an emaciated body, and they were virtually impossible to ignore. From the back, the truck looked like a mechanical version of Twiggy. Mario figured if he could buy that old Ghostbusters-style ambulance and pimp our ride, well…there's gold in them thar hills!

Time and again, Mario and I had talked for hours on the phone, sometimes deep into the wee hours of the morning, about the disturbing way that companies too-often treated their customers and, even worse, their employees.

"Man, if I ever had my own business," he'd say, "I'd treat the customers like gold. I really would." Me too, I'd chime in.

We hadn't been just two guys talking sports, playing sports, and selling at sporting events for decades, but two guys talking about how the sport of doing right by people was gone, like a fly ball hit deep into the Yankee night…. *See ya!* It seemed that most companies, especially the blue-chip ones, simply didn't give a rat's ass despite all the advertising and claims to try and disprove that. We both felt that the word loyalty would be eliminated from the dictionary in the near future.

C'mon, don't tell me you don't know what I mean!

Ever try getting compensated from the airlines for sitting on the tarmac for three hours or slogging your way through unintelligible and impossible to understand customer service reps to dispute a bill over the phone? Or trying to get a live customer at a cable company? What about someone to help you in Aisle 5 at Home Depot or—mercy me!—to show you to your seats at the Stadium? Remember when well-dressed, bow tie-wearing ushers at the Stadium used those fluffy mitts to wipe your seats off before you sat down? (It might've been around the time they re-signed druggie Steve Howe for another million-dollar go-round, and let the ushers go.)

Speaking of loyalty . . .

Recently, I wanted to check my Direct TV bill because it seemed a bit out of whack, so I called Direct TV. After wading through the usual phone options, I was subjected to:

CALLS MAY BE MONITORED FOR QUALITY PURPOSES and...PRESS 1 FOR THE LATEST MOVIE...PRESS 2 FOR A HAIRCUT AND SHAVE...PRESS 3 FOR A TRIM...OR HOLD ON FOR A LIVE OPERATOR WHILE LISTENING TO ELTON JOHN'S GREATEST HITS VOLUMES 1, 2 AND 3.

I met a guy once that worked at IBM. He worked in the computer lab tinkering away with hard drives, floppy disks, and motherboards. "Pretty cool," I said. "How'd you end up at IBM?" He made a funny face and rolled his eyes. He said he couldn't believe how many people ooohed and aaahed when he told them he worked for IBM. "If they only knew," he said, the negative tone as apparent as a poor internet connection.

Most people, heck, most of the world, had no idea what it was really like to work for IBM. There was constant mismanagement, which trickled down and reared its ugly head to both employees and consumers alike. And the working conditions. Oh my! "Nobody believes me. After all, it's I-B-M."

Um, yes I believe you. After all, I work for the Yankees. Well, my company, Centerplate, works for the Yankees and I work at the Stadium; ipso facto, that makes me a member of the Yankee Family. Yup, we're part of the Pride and Power and Class that's associated with the 26-time World Champions.

Did I tell you about the shithole that's the vendor's locker room?

Despite the Glory of the Pinstripes, despite the Headquarters for the Home Office of Major League Baseball being housed right here in the Bronx, at times working at the Stadium ain't no picnic, ain't no walk in the park.

At times, Gestapo tactics can do that to you.

Mario had simply had enough—and had been smitten with a unique business idea. Like me with comedy, he'd gotten a new girlfriend and planned to devote most of his attention to her. Little did we both realize how high maintenance she'd turn out to be.

* * *

Mario was on his way out and I was staying put, though I'd be a silent investment partner and part-time driver for Emergency Advertising. The parallels to OPERATION GRAMPRO were obvious. Unfortunately, I'd lose a lot more cash investing in Emergency Advertising, which despite an exciting concept, was done in after 9/11. After all, who really wanted to see another *ambulance*, 1959 or otherwise, following the nightmares that New York City faced with the horrific attack on the Twin Towers?

We'd both take solace in the fact that, in the end, we'd get a ton of publicity from the lost venture.

With millions of single people out there and millions of talented comics awaiting their big break, you have to create your own publicity once in a while to break into the Public Eye.

Both Mario and I would soon enjoy our first 15 Minutes of Fame.

* * *

We criss-crossed the five boroughs with our boxes of World Series programs, even crossed over into Nassau County, and soon realized we were in trouble, *big* trouble. People, forever skeptical, just don't buy things from people who come in from off the street with what they assume to be either suspect or stolen merchandise.

When was the last time you bought something from someone off the street, nickel bags notwithstanding?

Dejected, demoralized, and wiped out like a cocky surfer taking on a killer wave, I hit the sack in the wee hours of the morning. What should've been a celebration—we heard Jose Vizcaino's game-winning hit in the 12th inning for the Yankees on the car radio at 1:00 a.m.—felt more like I'd drowned in a dunk tank.

Step right up boys and girls! See the incredibly stupid vendors!

On January 3, 1973, George S. Steinbrenner III, that ol' Cleveland ship-builder, bought the New York Yankees from CBS for $10 million. The Bronx Zoo came to town shortly afterwards. You know all about the sideshows.

Somewhere along the way, the franchise's value ballooned to over a *billion* dollars, not including Alex Rodriguez's jockstrap.

Centerplate replaced Canteen Corporation shortly after my debut and ran the operations. The change in name and food prices might have been the only things Centerplate ever changed.

"I'm so tired of this place," Mario would say when the subject of working the eighth game of a ten-game homestand came up. "Don't get me wrong, Steve. You know I love this job. But how can people be suspended for wearing their badge inside out? How can our jobs be threatened when they won't let us put ice in our trays even though the beer is warm? How could management make a vendor pay for a new uniform because he didn't know they were fumigating the locker room before the next homestand and vendors didn't work the last one? How could they have taken the

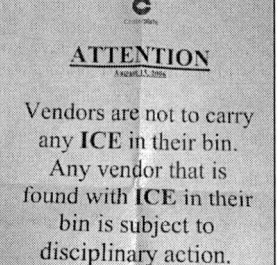

ATTENTION
August 15, 2006

Vendors are not to carry any **ICE** in their bin. Any vendor that is found with **ICE** in their bin is subject to disciplinary action.

clothes out of the locker and thrown them into a big pile for *anyone* to claim? Wouldn't you think if they clipped the locks on your locker and took out your stuff, that they'd *save* the stuff? Put it in a bag with your name on it?"

Either pay for a new uniform or you can't work…

And some of the fans! You'd think the vendors were Public Enemy #1. While the majority of them are good sports, there are the usual loud-mouths and jerks that give all fans a bad rap. I've been cursed at, spit at, purposely bumped into, and usually it's me having to explain *my* actions to The Penguin.

All right, Lazarus, we got this complaint…

Guys have been suspended for asking a fan, "Excuse me, please?" to move his leg a notch so they could get by in the front row rather than walking an extra 250 feet around three aisles with a blast-furnace hot dog bin on a sweltering day.

Yo man! I ain't movin' shit! I paid big bucks for this seat! Go fucking 'round the aisle.

Rarely would management side with the vendor.

We got letters…

It would get worse through the years. Like the time I was suspended three games.

BEER & ALCOHOL POLICIES #5
…You must ID anyone who appears to be under the age of 40.

Now think about that rule for a second, won't ya? How can a vendor be suspended for what can only be termed a judgment call? Isn't it an opinion if a person looks a certain age? If a vendor felt there was no need to check an ID, there was no need to check an ID. Now if the person happened to be under drinking age…Whoa Nelly!

Often Centerplate created their own version of The Sting. They'd send out employees to buy beer from vendors to see if they were asking for proper ID. Often, these employees would buy a beer and, even, tip the guy. (How screwed up is that? Here's a tip for ya, pardner. Sorry about the ensuing trouble you're about to have heaped upon your dumb ass!) Is it possible, or even probable, that these employees they sent to buy beer looked under 40? Sure.

But that's not the point. (Forget about the fact that they were of drinking age.)

The Penguin would call you into her office and sit you down. She'd commence with the day's current events, her chair squeaking under her onslaught.

So the story is, Sonny, a couple of spotters saw you selling beer to someone that was under 40 and you didn't check them for ID.

Who, me?

We're gonna have to suspend you.... See ya next homestand.

Wait, wait! I've been checking IDs all day! Who was it?

Sorry there, Sonny. I'm not allowed to divulge that information. It's Top Secret. Classified Information.

Hold on, hold on! I'm being suspended without even seeing my accuser? Obviously, I thought the person was over 40!

Pursed lips verge on becoming a smug smile. The Penguin strengthens her jaw muscles to hold it in check. She's got to be thinking *Got Ya!*

I suffered through that ignominy, and so did countless others.

In this Kangaroo Court, the verdict stands. Wonder how the rule *You must ID anyone who appears to be under the age of 40* would go over in a real court.

Is it any reason that Mario wanted out? So, at times, I was just as disillusioned with the job as he was.

By eight o'clock that OPERATION GRAMPRO evening, the car was finally crammed with the boxes of Subway Series programs—and by eleven o'clock, having traveled to Manhattan, Queens, and Long Island, and with the Yankees and Mets still playing, we weren't doing too well with the programs.

This can't be! How can we be turned down every single time, at every single juncture? How can people not want these? Don't they know they can't get these programs anywhere else? How can everyone be so ga-ga for the Subway Series but not want to buy the Official Program?

People regarded us as bums approaching them for spare change or junkies in need of a handout. We walked into bars and clubs, restaurants, Starbucks, grocery stores, 7-11s, Dunkin Donuts, White Castle, pizza shops, a Greyhound Bus Depot, and a bunch of other places only to be turned away like gate-crashers at a nude ball. We spoke with people on the street, people out for an evening stroll, a young couple walking their dog...but no one wanted a program. We hovered around the entranceway of supermarkets, walked into 24-hour laundromats and pool halls with televisions blaring the game, fans intoxicated by the action and nada, zilch. We walked into Jillians, an entertainment center on Long Island, where our voices were drowned out by the cacophony of bowling pins and pinball machines, "no thanks" echoing in our ears like the sound of a jackhammer.

People everywhere were wearing Mets and Yankees apparel: jerseys, shirts, jackets, warm-up suits. Some of the fans even had charm bracelets and watches and necklaces and every kind of attire you could imagine— and no one bought a program.

What the fuck?

Not only did they not buy one, they scattered from us like tenpins before we even approached, as if we had rubber-stamped signs on our foreheads reading SCAMMER. The looks we'd seen, the looks that had been shot back at us when we approached, were those given the homeless man begging for change on a street corner. Their eyes said what their lips didn't: stay away from me!

The lepers are coming! The lepers are coming!

How could this be? We had something that they couldn't possibly do without, and couldn't possibly have unless they were at the game *that night*, and the game was still on! The beauty of the idea was that they'd have the program while they were watching the game. "Yo, man, I already told you, get the fuck away from me!"

Some people would take a program, flip through it, and then hand it back. "How do I know that's not a fake program?"

Others were a little more blunt.

"Twenty bucks? It says ten dollars on the cover! Get outta here."

All this—and what made me feel worse was that not only was I going to lose a ton of money, but I could've made big bucks if I'd just worked the damn game!

I hadn't been in a fistfight since I was a kid but we came close on several occasions to getting into serious scuffles. I could see the headlines now had things gotten just a bit more out-of-control:

YANKEE STADIUM VENDORS SLAIN IN QUEENS
Beaten, left for dead selling Subway Series programs

Police report two men were found dead on a Flushing street corner last night among 40 empty boxes of Yankees and Mets World Series programs by an elderly woman walking her dog. Their battered and bruised bodies were littered with remnants of what appeared to be glossy pages from the FALL CLASSIC programs.
The Yankees beat the Mets in the series opener, 4-3, in 12 innings, a five-hour affair that was the longest game in World Series history. It was eternity, however, for two hapless souls.

"My poodle, Ruthie, was just sniffing around these parts looking for a place to do her business," said the woman, who requested anonymity. Interestingly, she was wearing a vintage Babe Ruth No. 3 jersey. "I don't want people knowing I'm a Yankee fan living in Queens," said the woman, an old housecoat draped over her frail body to ward off the late-night chill. "That's one reason I wear my jersey only when I walk my dog after midnight. It's dangerous being a Yankee fan—especially this time of year in Queens.

"Suddenly," she said, "Ruthie was barking like a real animal—I'd never heard her like that—she's such a sweet old thang, ain't she?—and that's when she burrowed into those empty boxes and saw those poor boys..."

Police admit they have few solid leads in the baffling case. "They were just left for dead," said one veteran cop. "It looks like whoever did this showed no mercy; they were really in a bad way. One of the guys had a nose that that was bashed in—possibly with a tire iron—and, incredibly, it was still huge!"

"The only things we found on them were some loose singles, their Yankee Stadium IDs, and a pair of $8.50 beer badges," said a detective assigned to the case. "It's really a shame," he offered. "Imagine paying that much for a beer!"

The dead were identified as...

Dejected from being rejected and ejected from a series of establishments, we stopped off at a diner, to wallow in our sorrows over small bites of food and drink. Then we drove back to my house where we sat slumped on the stoop of my apartment, still not knowing what the hell to do. My Honda sat nearby, the boxes of programs neatly stacked in the back of it, the same amount we'd started with six hours before. We sold *one* program the entire time and I honestly don't rememer who it was to.

The street was utterly silent.

At varying intervals, a lone car would pass under a street lamp, the driver's face illuminated by the sodium arc. Most of the drivers looked dazed in the early morning glow, much like we did.

Then Mario had another brainstorm. "Why don't we just bring the programs back to the Stadium and resell 'em?" he said.

"Whaddaya mean?"

"Just what I said."

With the dawn of a new day, we were going to make like Pierce Brosnan in the *Thomas Crowne Affair* and return the goods from whence they came. All we had to do was figure a way to smuggle a zillion World Series programs back into the Stadium. Maybe we could cut our losses after all. Or maybe I could just slit my wrists.

Overnight, another brainstorm hit me: we put 16 boxes up for sale on eBay and were lucky to sell them for $2000 (or half price) in a BUY IT NOW auction. With the other 24 boxes we tried to reverse what we had done the day before. I got a hand truck from the Stadium, loaded up the boxes from my car and brought them back in for Game 2. Nobody said anything when we slipped in through a side gate. How could they? We were vendors in uniform and we were selling programs.

I took a scorecard gate and Mario hit the seats and by the end of the game, we had incredibly sold them all, managing to cut our losses significantly.

The two bright guys from the Bronx, the street-savvy ones that knew how to make a quick buck as always, ended up as the only vendors not to make a dime in the Subway Series. Mario's emboldened stance with his new business venture had started all this OPERATION GRAMPRO (a variation of the word 'program') nonsense, but this time there was some light at the end of the tunnel—in more ways than one.

Mario knew the business wasn't going to make it and soon started cutting his losses, which in the end would total an astonishing half-million dollars. Nine ambulances and one hearse would also end up as part of the carnage. Mario said he had fun designing the business and starting it from the ground up, but he was no salesman. The economy didn't help, either.

In the end, he was a beaten man. "I only sell hot dogs well," he said. "And maybe I can write a little, too."

Two years later, during the 2002 baseball playoffs, the Daily News ran an article by columnist Denis Hamill that thrust me into not only the local spotlight but the national one, as well.

From there, I took the show on the road.

"TODAY I CONSIDER MYSELF THE LUCKIEST BEER MAN ON THE FACE OF THE EARTH"

read the sign on the 12' high car.

The '59 Cadillac Ambulance and Me at Yankee Stadium would make headlines around the nation and land me a few minutes on FOX, ABC, and CNN. *Good Day New York* would spotlight my work at the Stadium and in a local comedy club in a segment on both their morning and evening news that juxtaposed both jobs. There I was, one second at the Stadium in the stands with fans thirsting for my beer, and in the next instant I was seen entertaining a full house at Pip's Comedy Club in Brooklyn, the audience thirsting for laughs.

Cool.

Mario would end up on the *Today Show* advertising for a wife on Valentine's Day 2003. He received thousands of emails from eligible women. (He said most of them were probably cross-dressers so he only went out with a few. "They dressed well," he said.)

Following the playoffs, in which the Yankees were eliminated from a chance at the World Series by the California Angels, I got a bunch of calls from comedy clubs in the metropolitan area that asked for the availability of The Beer Man.

I told them I'd only work if they built me a bathroom.

* * *

No matter what it is you're seeking publicity for—a break into the big-time as a stand-up comic, a wife, or just to let the world know you've got something unique you'd like to show them or possibly sell them, the ways to get attention are as endless as space.

In the entertainment industry, you can hire a publicist, do it yourself or use a combination of both. I've done all three—and tasted both success and failure with each. I've amassed a pretty thorough press kit that includes my business card, a little about me, my career accomplishments (I left out the story about Yonkers Raceway), a few pictures and vitals (single, well hung), some articles written about me, and standard resume-like things. In my press kit I've also included a five minute DVD of some of my funnier bits. (There's a pair of Yankee tickets in the press kit, as well, in case they didn't think the bits were *that* funny.)

In this day and age of instant gratification—*Mommy, mommy I want that three-hundred dollar cell phone with Web-cam features! But honey, you're only in kindergarten!*—it's incumbent for any performer to have their own website. It's a "live" extension of your press kit. Best of all, the site can be viewed 24 hours a day, seven days a week, 365.

On my website—SteveLazarus.com and YankeeBeerMan.com, which are linked together—I have comedy club performances, a couple of commercials I made, my bio, feature articles, pictures, a counter showing the number of women I've slept with (it's updated daily), and much more.

MEDIA ALERT
10/3/2005
AVAILABLE FOR INTERVIEWS

Contact Steve Lazarus
(917) 304-8366
comiclaz1@aol.com

<u>Yankee Stadium Beer Man Slings the Suds and the Jokes</u>

New York City—Yankee Stadium vendor, Steve Lazarus, celebrates his 29th anniversary making fans laugh in the seats at the ballpark and at Comedy Clubs around the country as well. Lazarus, 47, uses his "day job" as a Yankee Stadium beer vendor as a source for many of his stand-up comedy routines. The Beer Man is one of the highlights at the House that Ruth Built, keeping audiences alive at the big ballpark in the Bronx, especially during this month of playoff games.

Slinging suds came before slinging jokes for The Bronx native and lifetime Yankees fanatic. In 1977, Steve, then a college student, started vending at Yankee Stadium. He was vendor # 2711 and he felt like he was in the minor leagues. Today, he's vendor # 55 and the Man—*The Beer Man*. In 1995, Steve embarked on a double-play—and, in time, fulfilled his ultimate fantasy. "I always wanted to do what Robert Klein and George Carlin did for a living," he says. "I was always witty and clever. I could make people laugh. I thought, what better life could there be than being *The Beer Man* at Yankee Stadium and a stand-up comedian?"

Steve's comedy career started at Don't Tell Mama's in Manhattan—and, naturally, he mined "sales experience" for material. Steve says sometimes he feels like a woman with big breasts when he's selling beer. "The straps dig into my shoulders, my back is always killing me, and all the guys, well . . . they just stare at my cups."

Today, Steve's hilarious tales of his grandstand adventures have convulsive audiences across the country, from Atlantic City to Las Vegas—where he performs a few weeks each year—taking notice as he pitches one gem after another. Steve has shared the stage with the likes of superstars Ray Romano, Robert Klein, and Kevin James. But don't expect to see Steve anywhere other than Yankee Stadium this week. He never books dates in October. "I can't let anything get in the way of Yankee postseason," he insists.

Steve is also working on an autobiography about his beer vendor/ comic experiences expected to be published in 2006.

Okay, so I fell a little behind schedule on the book deal.

This press release was used in one of the times I hired a publicist. It was culled from a number of releases I had written through the years and updated to reflect my "star status"—and sent over the internet via "Wireless Web News Flash."

I always figured what better road to take than playoff time to try and get national attention. Plus, just about anything the Yankees do makes national headlines in the sports world. The funny thing is that I've done something like this a few times myself on a smaller scale and, like anything else, I've had a few hits, a few near-misses, and even struck out a number of times. All along, I learned a thing or two that made me much more aware of what I'll do differently the next time.

What's important in hiring a publicist is that the good ones have certain connections in the business and that can be key to real over-the-top and, possibly, long-term exposure. My main goal is to be on television because the exposure can make you an "overnight" sensation and you become a draw—and more of a chick magnet than I already am.

As Peter Bales says, "Now you're holding the hammer."

On some television outlets, like Fox, I've pitched the same thing to different people many times and was on their show twice in just a few years.

In 2006, Fox 5 did a live remote from my brother's house in Suffern, New York, and taped the Lazarus clan rooting for the Pinstripes as they took on the Angels in California in a playoff game—while we were celebrating Rosh Hashanah. We used a shofar to root on our favorite team, the cameras tracking our every move for the 11:00 p.m. news.

The Rabbi couldn't make it; he was stuck in Philly.

I've been interviewed on the *Mike and the Mad Dog* radio program on WFAN in New York, the # 1 Sports Talk show in the nation at the time; played a beer vendor in a skit on the aptly-titled *Last Call with Carson Daly*; and was featured in a two-page article in the *Village Voice*.

For those on a limited budget—who isn't?—hiring a publicist can be expensive: I've spent anywhere from $500 to $2500 for just a week to a few weeks' work. Sometimes, I've been interviewed by a number of radio stations so off the beaten path, that only farmers in Iowa or lumberjacks in Saskatchewan heard it.

Who knows, however, what little thing will turn out big? Who knows who will be listening to your interview in Kalamazoo, Michigan, or watching you at 2:00 a.m. in Dubuque, Iowa?

On the first day of the playoffs every year (luckily the Yankees have had a good playoff run in recent times), I would drop off a few press kits and news releases in the Stadium Press Box—another advantage of a Man in Uniform—and usually get a few calls from the assembled media; it might amount to anything from a blurb in the *New York Times* or *New York Post* or my favorite Spanish daily, *El Diario*.

Si!

The press kit may even lead to an article down the road in the *Daily News* about a vendor that makes his own "Beer Batter Chicken."

Sad to say, I never made it to "The Martha Stewart Show" as the only thing she was serving when this article came out was jail time.

As an entertainer, you try to sell yourself whenever you work, be it the smallest dump or the biggest hall. You build a website, make yourself a nice little business card, design an effective press kit and continually update each and every thing you do to make yourself better—and that's *besides* your act. You drop a word here, a word there; you send press releases and press kits and volunteer to do a lot of things that others would never consider doing. You hope that something will stick to the wall, that somewhere the Ripple Effect will take place and one job will turn into another and another . . . and another.

Today it seems like everyone is trying to get their 15 Minutes of Fame and continually thinking outside the box in ways to get it; the trick is once you get that attention, to make it last—and to possibly turn those rare chances into a lifetime of good fortune in the industry.

And maybe one day get a chance to write a best-selling book about it.

NINTH INNING

Coming Full Circle

Yankee Stadium is often referred to as baseball's great cathedral, its center field regarded as hallowed ground.

- LARRY MCSHANE, DAILY NEWS

ON TUESDAY, NOVEMBER 13, 2007, I sat down at my usual greasy spoon in Bayside for my morning coffee. I turned the page of the *New York Post* and I felt like I had just hit the lottery. Before I even read the story, I called Mario.

"You're not going to believe this," I said.

"Uh, huh," he said. "Go ahead." His tone indicated that he'd heard me say something like this before.

"I'm going to change the name of the book," I said.

"*What are you talking about?*" he said defensively. Mario had given me the name for the book—and was quite proud of it, though admittedly, at first, I had my concerns.

"Yeah, I'm gonna call it 'The *Popes* and Me at Yankee Stadium.'"

According to the paper, The Pope was coming to Yankee Stadium the following April to say Mass. The 79th All-Star Game was scheduled three months later, in July.

My time at Yankee Stadium was about to come full circle.

* * *

It seemed fitting that my vending career at Yankee Stadium would come full circle in 2008, the last year of the original House that Ruth Built, with a new Yankee Stadium under construction across the street. It was being built to the standards of the original Stadium built in 1923,

145

though this one would have all the modern and technological amenities. A new era was set for Opening Day 2009 when history would be revisited and the Bronx would turn back the clock to a more peaceful time (though there would be scanners).

The 79th All-Star game was held here for the last time, marking my 31st anniversary as a vendor, and Pope Benedict XVI celebrated Mass for the last large-scale Catholic celebration. There were 200,000 requests for tickets to celebrate with the Pope but only 57,000 seats.

None of the people attending Papal Mass ever saw The Pope and Me, nor any other vendor for that matter. No vendor ever knew why there was no vending that day, but I wonder: how did the counter workers at the stands handle 57,000 hungry people?

Nope, you can't come into the ballpark if you're not working. It says so right there in General Rule #23. I was very upset I wouldn't be working and I thought, there goes the ending to my book!

I watched the pomp and circumstance on television and was amazed how they turned a baseball field into such a place of grace and beauty. But then again, isn't part of baseball just that? I was amazed at the stage set-up, how organized and stunning the pageantry of it all was, and the seriousness of the crowd. I kept thinking that this was a big event at the Stadium and I should be there working.

In truth, this Jewish vendor would've loved to have been there from not only an historical standpoint but as a bookend to my life and times as the Beer Man at Yankee Stadium.

Plus, I could've made a few bucks too—not like back in 1979. Unless I was stuck selling *Hebrew National* hot dogs again.

* * *

The All-Star game had its own pageantry, as well. Forty-nine Hall of Famers were assembled at the Stadium, and I couldn't help being swept up in the tidal wave of emotions that so many felt when the superstars converged on the infield lawn. There were legendary Yankees like Yoga Berra, Whitey Ford, and Reggie Jackson. Superstars Willie Mays, Hank Aaron, Brooks Robinson, Lou Brock, Steve Carlton, Rollie Fingers, Bob Gibson, and the Horse Whisperer, Wade Boggs, were also among the honorees.

Many hearty old-timers like me couldn't help but get emotional. Out there on the field were players we grew up with, players we rooted for, players we desperately rooted against, stars we looked for in box scores or kept track of in the *Sporting News* or *Sports Illustrated*. They all were a big part of the tapestry of my youth.

And here they were again.

I read that people paid huge ticket prices for the 79th All-Star Game, some seats going for thousands of dollars. They would certainly get their money's worth. I made nearly $800 selling commemorative All-Star programs both before and after the game, and beer during it. The game, the longest All-Star game in history, nearly a five-hour affair, finally ended at 1:38 a.m. the next morning. I was sorry to see it all end. It was as if the spirits of Yankee Stadium didn't want to let go. And neither did I.

It was something, however, that took place during the anthem that made me think about how much things had changed since I first started here as a raw 19-year-old rookie.

I happened to gaze skyward towards the Stadium rooftop, where powerful lights bathed the field in a radiant glow, and did a double-take. There perched on the rooftops, strung along the top where the old facades used to be, stood an army of New York City Police sharpshooters, guns at the ready, should anyone think about doing something a bit more radical than just excessive drinking in the stands.

Chills ran down my spine when a Stealth B-52 Bomber roared overhead soon after. I felt safe, proud.

It's amazing, I thought, how the world had changed so much since 9/11 and since I first started here in 1977. I then picked up my beer tray and was off to the races.

*　　*　　*

Someone once said that time moves on, and the closing curtain of Yankee Stadium and the dawn of a new era would soon be upon us. Kate Smith would sing "God Bless America" one final time, Frank Sinatra would do likewise with "New York, New York," and Mariano Rivera would shatter a few more bats before adding one final save.

Time marches on.

It does for vendors, as well. At warp speed.

POST GAME SHOW

ON AUGUST 16, 2006, ground was broken for the new Yankee Stadium on the site of Macombs Dam Park, across the street from where I spent nearly four decades working. Of course, Yankees' principal owner, George M. Steinbrenner was there as were Mayor Michael Bloomberg, Governor George Pataki, and a dozen other dignitaries. Yogi Berra and Alex Rodriguez were also on hand. They were all captured shoveling dirt out of a hole as if they were clearing their respective driveways following a mild snowfall.

The scene was accompanied by a cacophony of electronic flashes, whirring camera shutters, and laughter from the assembled dignitaries. There were a number of speeches made, most of them talking about Yankee tradition. They spoke of how everyone—fans, players, New York City, heck, the world!—stood to benefit.

Already, many of the benefits of the new park were apparent in the neighborhood: a new park had been constructed where before only a parking lot stood. And it was more than just a park! It was a synthetic turf field replete with a three-lane running track, exercise bars, dugout seating, benches, and *newness*.

A few blocks away, a massive shopping center, hailed as the "Gateway Center at Bronx Terminal Market," sprung up in no time, where before only weeds and abandoned buildings stood. I was destined to be here, in the new Yankee Stadium, the one that would mimic the original—but with all the modernity that technology could muster.

The white facades, known the world over, are here once again. They're *everywhere* in the new Yankee Stadium, unlike in the old, revamped Stadium. The familiar bleachers are here, separated by "The Black." And, of course, the *newness*.

There are dozens of retail shops, a food court with delectables from all over the world, and concession stands selling all the must-have Yankee gear and apparel. There's an expansive concourse and an enclosed mall featuring the Hard Rock Cafe, both a sports and martini bar, and a steakhouse. There's an art gallery and museum, as well. All in the hopes of luring people into the South Bronx, even when there is no game going on.

Wow, a new Yankee Stadium after all these years. Where else would I want to be? Where else would I *expect* to be?

Gone are the box seats with cushions held together with duct tape. Gone are the small, barely-able-to-squeeze-by aisles where I couldn't avoid banging into someone. Gone, too, are the lockers in the locker room from Hell. New beer bins, new freezers to keep the beer cold, everything new, new, new.

Here was a fresh start, like a team at the beginning of a season. No runs, hits, errors. I'm keeping that first ten dollar bill that a customer used to pay for the $9.50 beer; it's scotch-taped to my computer hutch. Here I am in the new home of the New York Yankees in this swanky, state-of-the-art $1.3 billion dollar palace.

The vinyl and plastic on the new chairs shine. The floors, like the cliché goes, are clean enough to eat off of. I can smell the freshly painted walls. Some of the Stadium furniture, like the scorecard portables, are still in plastic wraps.

Virgin all the way.

It was probably like this when the old Yankee Stadium was renovated back in 1974-75, before I started. How long did it take before it fell into disarray, culminating on April 13, 1998 when a 500-pound concrete and steel beam came crashing down on a loge seat, four hours prior to that evening's game?

A new Yankee Stadium? For years it was just talk, talk, talk. Now it's more than talk, more than a dream. It's reality.

For most.

As I write this, it's September 25, 2008, and the Yankees have just been eliminated from any post-season play for the first time since 1996.

While their fate has been sealed for the 2008 season, their new one is set for April 2009.

Unfortunately, the vendors don't have that same luxury.

Centerplate has already been told they're out at home; their contract has not been renewed for the 2009 season leaving the Yankees' new Field of Dreams a possible nightmare for some 400 workers.

The Yankees will be handling everything "in-house" at the new Yankee Stadium with Legends Hospitality Management, a new player in the sports industry. Interestingly, one of LHM's principals, Dan Smith, was a vendor at the Stadium in 1977.

Hopefully, Mr. Smith will remember that.

Will those workers who supplement their regular incomes as teachers, actors, accountants, correction officers, office assistants, bartenders, messengers, truck drivers, or those just working their way through college, be left behind like a resin bag on the pitcher's mound at the end of the end of a game?

And what about the idiot that thinks he's a comedian? The guy that was supposed to sign a lucrative deal with CBS for syndication rights to *Hey Hotdog!* What will happen to his double-play combination?

* * *

Long ago, when my teacher, Mr. Rothman, asked me what the heck I wanted to do with the rest of my life, I told him: "I'd like to work outdoors and feed the hungry." Later on, I realized I wanted to tell a few jokes to go along with that.

Now if I'm not working at the new Yankee Stadium, how will I try out my material?

EXTRA INNINGS

TO INFINITY AND BEYOND

It ain't over till it's over!
-YOGI BERRA

September 26, 2014

NOW BATTING FOR THE YANKEES, number two, Derek Jeter ... number two ....

As I stood there amongst a sea of Yankee faithful in the final home game of the year, in a season in which the Yankees had long since been out of playoff contention, cheers rang out from the packed stadium crowd one last time for The Captain—DER-EK JEE-TER, DER-EK JEE-TER—as he sauntered to the plate with the score tied 5-5 against the Baltimore Orioles in the bottom of the ninth and a runner on second. It would be his last at-bat at the HOUSE THAT JETER BUILT (as one sign put it) in his storied 20-year pinstriped career.

The script is there, would be the way Yankees announcer Michael Kay would put it as Jeter moved into the batter's box, adjusted his elbow pads—*like me!*—took a few practice swings, and dug in ... with cheers straining towards a crescendo ....

And it was over in a split-second.

Jeter lined the first pitch hard just past a lunging Orioles first baseman and pinch-runner Antoan Richardson slid home safely as the Stadium erupted at Destiny's ending, and Jeter was mobbed by his teammates.

For Derek Jeter, his fantasy ending had been a reality.

Mine would be just a leetle different.

*   *   *

They're building a new stadium across the street? Geez. I thought they were building condos! is what I told a reporter that was interviewing some vendors for a *Daily News* article back in 2008, when there was that talk about the Yankees hiring all new vendors for an all new ballpark leaving us out in the old New York cold.

When negotiations were over and we were finally "allowed" to take the walk across the street with the rest of the Yankee brass in April 2009 —at a much-reduced pay-rate, of course—I thought of my man Barry Manilow: It looks like we made it.

And indeed we had. But not quite the way one would've liked.

The only people who like change are wet babies.
- MARK TWAIN

And so a new chapter in Yankee history had begun in a Stadium big enough to house Kennedy Airport, and so had mine—albeit with a number of sweeping changes.

No beer vending—or any vending for that matter!—in the hoity-toity, three-hunnert-dollars-and-up lower level seats. (The waiters and waitresses would tend to that; Um, sir, would you like a backrub with that?) We'd now wear "professional" uniforms designed with awkward pinstripes and the word VENDOR on the back in bold bad-ass lettering. (You mean that guy waving that box of Peanuts around going Get your nuts here! Big nuts here! is an undercover agent?)

Bottles of beer—sorry, Ma'am but NO you can't keep the cap! How do I know you won't fling it into Mariano Rivera's eye should he blow the save!—now costing as much as a pair of Nikes. More vendors in a smaller allotment of Stadium boundaries, making it seem at times like we were bumper cars at an amusement park. And, yes, the dawn of the IBM age at your local ballpark: a computerized vending system, one in which you now had to wait on a long line both coming and going before trying to make a buck; sorta like going through airport security without stripping into your civvies though you had to wait until Homeland Security says, uh, Sir? You can go now!

Heck, I even had to work in the upper deck for the first time in 20 years ... but, hey, at least we made it!

This and so much more. And your bonus prize, Mr. Lazarus and Company?

You're now gonna make *half* of what you used to.

Take it or leave it. Have a nice day.

* * *

The new Yankee Stadium, built at a cost of a gazillion dollars, was ultra-impressive and state of the art. While the fans might have loved the Yankees Museum featuring stars of the past like The Babe and Lou and Mickey and Reggie and Whitey and hundreds of balls—no, not like the ones Yolanda Vega pulls—signed by Yankees past and present, or marveled at a sparkling array of World Series rings and Thurman Munson's original locker, or buying a Peter Max or LeRoy Neiman sports-themed print to an oversized New York Yankees beanbag chair in the shape of a glove for a mere $995 at a number of specialty retail shops, the vendors were stunned with how many different places to eat or drink there now were! Beers were offered from around the world with all kinds of funny names like *Blue Moon* and *Batch 19 Lager, Leinenkugel's Summer Shandy* and *Crispin Cider,* and my personal fave, *Checker Cab Blonde Ale.* You want a bimbo with that? There were all different types of craft beers, as well.

Really, how could a lowly vendor with one lukewarm bottle of Bud compete with that?

Jobs with a puny salary for two-hundred, Alex.

Sure, the aisles might have been so enormous that I might not bonk people in the head every other run down one (though they weren't too wide if they stiffed me for a tip), and there were no unsightly beams to obstruct fan views like I'd personally experienced in the old Stadium with Dear Old Dad, now even the seats were padded, making for a very hemorrhoid-friendly establishment for the geriatric set. *I useta pay fifty cents for a box seat, ain't that right Mabel?* So life was good for the fans, but as for the vendors, the Gravy Train had been derailed.

And how many fans even sat in their seats for most of the game to even buy from the vendors? What was I supposed to do, sling the suds and the jokes to fans while they were waiting on line to buy *a two-foot long* cheesesteak—dubbed the "Tape Measure"—that cost as much as a tank of gas, and probably gave you some, too.

There was so much to do at the new Stadium besides watching baseball, that many of the seats remained empty even when the Stadium was sold out. I mean, who wouldn't want to get a shave or a trim at the barbershop or buy some dinosaur-sized steak at the butcher shop in-between pitches? And besides, while you were purchasing that Gucci alligator bag at Yanks Fifth Ave., you could catch the game on the tractor-trailer sized televisions right over there. And there. And there.

Toto, I don't think we're in Kansas anymore.

Sometimes it seemed as though there just *happened* to be a baseball game going on here at the mall.

The new Stadium and all its highfalutin accoutrements wasn't the only change 2009 ushered in. The Yankees, always known for spending money and winning, signed the top three free agents on the market that winter: CC Sabathia, A.J. Burnett and Mark Teixeira. With their help and A-Rod's surprisingly clutch postseason hitting, along with huge contributions from what became known as the "Core Four" (Derek Jeter, Andy Pettitte, Mariano Rivera and Jorge Posada), the Yankees went on to win the World Series in 2009. It was the 27th in their incredible history and the seventh one I'd seen.

While the old Yankee Stadium hosted the occasional special event such as a concert or a college football game or even *The Pope and Me at Yankee Stadium,* the new one became the Hot Spot for other sports—*ice hockey anyone?*—as well as arts, entertainment, and more.

There was Madonna and Me at Yankee Stadium, Paul McCartney and Me at Yankee Stadium, Jay-Z and Me at Yankee Stadium, and even Pastor Joel Osteen and Me at Yankee Stadium. After all, what better place is there to talk about the Goodness of God than at such a revered, heavenly place like Yankee Stadium?

Though my fondest memories of my time as a vendor since 1977 were across the street where a beautiful Olympic-sized track and playground now stood, I found a fondness for this New White House as well.

For a while.
Until it was time to retire. Or, like Alex Rodriguez, *had* to retire.

* * *

Saturday, July 16, 2016

As I walked out of the eerily quiet Stadium into the sweltering early evening, unable to make it past the fourth inning because my neck had stiffened to the point where just saying *Yo Beer! Beer Man Here!* was downright painful, and my ankle continuing to swell after a bad misstep in the upper deck, I saw that the Yankees, the under .500 Yankees, hitless to that point against Red Sox knuckleballer Steven Wright—no joke—were limping and struggling along just like me . . .

That weekend was significant for me as it was my fortieth anniversary as a vendor for the Yankees, having started back in 1977 at the old Yankee Stadium for the All-Star game. I always felt that if I could hit that significant milestone, it might convince voters that I was worthy of being in the VENDORS HALL OF FAME (coming soon to a computer near you) and having a plaque in my honor.

STEVE LAZARUS WORKED 40 YEARS AT YANKEE STADIUM AND WAS KNOWN AS THE WORLD'S MOST INTERESTING BEER MAN. HE MADE WORLDWIDE HEADLINES IN 2003 WHEN HE SAID THAT BEING THE BEER MAN IS LIKE BEING A BIG BREASTED WOMAN. I'VE ALWAYS GOT THE STRAPS DIGGING INTO MY SHOULDERS, MY BACK IS ALWAYS KILLING ME, AND ALL THE GUYS STARE AT MY CUPS.

UNFORTUNATELY, STEVE WORKED UNTIL THOSE STRAPS CAUSED JUST TOO MUCH PAIN IN HIS SHOULDERS, HE SUFFERED FROM HERNIATED DISCS IN HIS SPINE, DEVELOPED CARPAL AND CUBITAL TUNNEL SYNDROME AND ARTHRITIS IN THE HIPS, HAD TENNIS ELBOW IN BOTH ARMS, AND A FRONTAL LOBOTOMY LEFT HIM WITH A BIG UGLY HOLE IN HIS HEAD— WHICH REALLY TURNED OFF MOST FANS, THOUGH THE DRUNK ONES DIDN'T CARE AND WOULD *STILL* BUY A BEER FROM HIM.

AMONG HIS CAREER HIGHLIGHTS . . .

I'd suffered through and worked in pain many times before, sometimes feeling like the Real Life version of *Operation!*—TAKE OUT WRENCHED ANKLE or REMOVE FUNNY BONE—but never like this.

As I crossed the street to the parking garage, a northbound IRT x train rumbling overhead jarring my bones, I realized this was something serious. I knew the ankle would eventually heal, but the neck? If truth be told, I was pretty nervous. When you sell beer and tell jokes for a living, well if it was going to pain me to speak, this was seriously no laughing matter.

The following night I watched the Yankees and Red Sox on ESPN from the 'comfort' of my living room couch, and hated every minute of it, even though the Yankees won. After all, when you can watch the rivalry to end all rivalries—one that first started in 1901, involved legendary figures, Hollywood storylines, and a tattered David Ortiz jersey buried and unearthed from the foundation of the new Yankee Stadium and eventually sold on eBay for $175,000—for free and make a buck while you're at it, well I wanted to be there. What Yankee fan wouldn't? And for as long as I could remember, I always was.

And now I wasn't.

Rats!

* * *

"Okay, now lie on your left side, and slowly turn your head towards me," Dr. Simon told me, gently holding my head and neck as I did so. I imagined it looking like a bent corkscrew. "Uh-huh, good, good. Does that hurt at all?"

"Do I earn bonus points if I say no?"

The doc offered a crooked smile. He then probed the area like he was mining for gold.

"Uh . . . We're gonna need to take some X-rays here . . ."

* * *

A half-hour later, I faced Dr. Doom and stark X-rays of my neck on a huge backlit screen. A part of it looked like an accordion with crushed keys. I didn't have to be a medical genius to see that there was something wrong, very wrong.

There were times in the past where my body was so wracked with pain, but I'd get a cortisone shot in my elbow or in my hip and voila! I was fine for the time being. *Ahh, the miracles of modern medicine,* I'd think. Yankee Stadium here I come!

But not this time.

This time I needed neck surgery—and ultimately would end up with a titanium plate in my head. Of course this meant that I'd never vend again, because I'd never be able to get past the full body scanner that the vendors had to go through to enter the Stadium without all the alarms going off—and a SWAT team surrounding me with bazookas aimed at my noggin.

All to sell a nine-dollar beer or a bottle of water for five bucks.

LAST CALL

My vending career wasn't supposed to end this way. After thousands of games patrolling and plodding and pounding the pavement desperately seeking sales, starting with soda in 1977 and graduating to peanuts and then ballpark franks (they weren't always so plump when you cooked them) and then a case of beer with a full complement of ice that made it feel like I was hauling around a redwood tree, I planned on working at least of couple of more championship seasons before I was unceremoniously cut down by a cartilage-eating Pac-Man; a devouring little fella that silently chomped away at my flesh for the last five decades at the Stadium.

I'd always wanted to retire on my own terms, wanted to be like Mariano or Jorge Posada or Derek and leave when I was ready, have my palatial estate waiting on the Florida coast, construction workers putting the finishing touches on the white facades that bordered the grounds, my Sea Ray anchored in the warm breeze, set to cruise along the shimmering Gulf. I figured I'd retire and live off my great memories—and a few book sales and autograph signings at comedy shows and baseball conventions. And royalties from The Pope and *Me at Yankee Stadium* documentary.

But life throws you a folly floater once-in-a-while and I ended up crawling back to my home dugout.

DO IT TO ME ONE MORE TIME

Yup, I long to sell one more beer to a fan and hear him say, "Here's a ten; keep it." I wouldn't mind giving one more fan directions to the upper deck—*See that long escalator over there?*—or tell them which bathroom that's the "least crowded." I'd love to hear more fans ask more silly questions, some totally knocking me for a loop: *Do you know where I could get some saline solution? Do they have baked squid at the Hard Rock? Do you know if they sell penis rings with the Yankee insignia on them?*

Or my personal fave: *Hey, do you get to hang out with the players?*

Sure, I tell them. *I have Derek and Alex and Andy on speed dial.*

I want to hear the collective shout of 50,000 Yankee diehards shouting Boston Sucks! just one more time. Or hear the Bleacher Creatures serenade an opposing team's right fielder.

And just once more I'd like to work alongside my long-time fellow vendors; be a part of the Animal House-like locker room one more time; be a part of the camaraderie, the backslapping, and the silliness that takes place when you stick a hundred men from all walks of life into a locker room as big as an oversized storage room.

But *Que Sera, Sera.*

CHECK OUT TIME

About ten days after I worked my final game, I received my last paycheck in the mail. I'd earned $35.00 for selling one case of beer, and figured I'd have enough left over after taxes for a few gallons of gas.

Maybe.

My final check of $0.00 put the kibosh on that.

I'd forgotten about union dues.

* * *

THE POPE AND ME AT YANKEE STADIUM

So here it was: I'd been a Yankee Stadium vendor since 1977 and was about to become Joe Average Fan again; an ordinary spectator with an AARP card. If I wanted to see my beloved Yankees in-person now, I'd have to buy a ticket like everyone else. Hopefully no idiot vendor would bonk me on the head if I didn't give him a good tip!

* * *

In 2014, when I watched Derek Jeter take the microphone and thank the fans for making his time in pinstripes so special, I thought how tough it must be to say goodbye to a job you've had for so long—like Jeter, I was just a teenager when I started here—having worked, in essence, your entire adult life in the same place. How does one say goodbye without a lump forming in your throat the size of a pitcher's mound?

I remember the way my favorite show M*A*S*H ended and kept thinking how cool it would be if I could do something like that on the scoreboard—but I had an inkling the Yankees wouldn't go for it.

STEVE LAZARUS